Praise for *Disenchanted*

"In *Disenchanted*, Kaycie Hall examines love, friendship, motherhood, and desire with honesty and precision. This is a truly beautiful debut."
—Chelsea Hodson, author of *Tonight I'm Someone Else*

"Nobody gets disenchanted without first becoming enchanted—by a lover, a place, a language, or even one's own child. Kaycie Hall writes about those states with an immersive sense of atmosphere, sly humor, and the voluptuous tristesse of an old soul buckled into a young person's life. These essays are magic."
—Peter Trachtenberg, author of *The Twilight of Bohemia* and *Another Insane Devotion*

"What lurks under our enchantments with others? Kaycie Hall's *Disenchanted* is an earthquake that cracks open the hidden realities we all try to avoid. In the early days of motherhood, Hall tends to her new son while facing her past relationships: friends, fetuses, romances, therapists, strangers, her own body. You won't be able to look away from her reckonings, nor will you want to. May all our faultlines have this much discernment and levity as they start to rumble."
—Lexi Kent-Monning, author of *The Burden of Joy*

"Gestations, heartaches, triumphs, these mark the accruing minutes of a self under construction, that Hall, with such

luminous clarity, evokes, rebels against, and queries. *Disenchanted* reads like a diamond, the pressurized past turned into something brilliant. This is a magic book."
—Heidi Julavits, author of *Directions to Myself* and *The Folded Clock: A Diary*

Published by Autofocus Books
autofocusbooks.com

Essays/Literature
ISBN: 978-1-957392-50-9
Library of Congress Control Number: 2026938963

The events in this book reflect the author's recollection. Some names, locations and identifying factors have been changed to protect the privacy of those depicted. Dialogue has been recreated from the author's memory.

Cover design by Amy Wheaton

Disenchanted

Kaycie Hall

Autofocus Books
Easton, Pennsylvania

“You’ll never know what your mother went through.”

—Sarah Manguso

Table of Contents

Disenchanted

Once Upon a Time

Bluebeard

Open anything you want. Go anywhere you wish. But I absolutely forbid you to enter that little room, and if you open it so much as a crack, nothing will protect you from my wrath.

I once loved a man who lived in a duplex in New Orleans, sparsely furnished with a couch, a bed, a chair. A tiny kitchen with an empty refrigerator. He seduced me with letters, late-night phone calls, and hand-rolled cigarettes. In that little duplex, he left me alone while he worked late at a bar, locking me inside. Once, I cut my leg shaving but didn't notice until, standing on his white shower mat, a trickle of blood dripped down my leg into the fibers. I cut away the blood spot, afraid he would notice.

I started poking around the dark corners of our life together. I questioned his long absences and the pills that he kept acquiring for pain that should have faded. He threw his phone into the duplex wall, a hole in the plaster, maniacally laughing at my fear. My brother threatened to drive to New Orleans if necessary, to kill this Bluebeard if he ever again laid a hand on me.

My son has only just started sleeping in his crib, in his own room. We have once again gone through his naptime routine—diaper, sleep sack, sound machine, pacifier, cry cry cry. I pull the footstool from his rocking chair up to his crib. I stick my finger through the crib bars and he grips it furiously, tossing and turning. Even though he's the one behind the bars, it is I who am the captive. I sigh, open the book of fairy tales on my lap. I know this is one better suited for adults, but my son just wants to hear the soft tones of my voice as he searches for sleep.

Rumpelstiltskin

"The Devil told you that, the Devil told you!" the little man screamed, and in his rage he stamped his right foot so hard that it went into the ground and right up to his waist. Then in his fury he seized his left foot with both hands and tore himself in two.

My son is practicing rolling. Naptime seems to be his preferred time to practice, so I read as he rolls onto his belly, onto his back, onto his belly, onto his back. I hold one hand up to the bars to keep him from sticking his chunky legs through. He falls asleep, but I finish reading the story anyway. When I get to the last lines, I snap a photo of the page and send it to a friend. I type "what the fuck."

In the year after graduate school, I was involved with a man I thought I knew. We fell in love while I was living in France, pixelated faces on a computer screen holding us over until I returned. They say absence makes the heart grow fonder, but what about desire? Lust can easily be confused for love when the months stretch on and words hold the place of sex.

When I returned, we took a road trip. This is where his little fits began.

Sensing my boredom on the long drive, he became agitated. He shuffled through CDs, putting one in, playing a few seconds, ejecting it. Again and again. I was reading a book and looked up at him in askance. He looked at me defiantly, rolled down his window and threw the entire case of CDs onto the highway. "What the fuck," I thought, but I stayed quiet. I had learned to trust my instincts when a threat was near. Be sweet and gentle and he will back down.

The fits escalated to screaming phone calls, throwing things—books, empty pill bottles, piles of papers—in the house. I grew tired of making myself small and gentle. When his rage erupted, it was like he was torn in two, one half the man I had known and the other a petulant monster. I screamed back. I left.

Rapunzel

"Oh, please," he replied, "show some mercy for my deed, for I did it only because I had to. My wife got a look at your rapunzel from our window. Her craving for it was so great that she said she would die if I couldn't get it for her." The enchantress relented in her anger and said to the man: "If what you said is true, then I'm going to let you take as much rapunzel as you want back with you. But on one condition: You must hand over the child after your wife gives birth. I will take care of it like a mother, and it will not want for anything."

I am home alone today and my son is fussy. He wants only to be held, and I am at my wit's end. I put his nursing pillow on my lap, situating him on top, his head in the crook of my arm. It is late afternoon, our apartment is a mess. I am still wearing pajamas, my hair is sticky from little fingers grabbing and pulling out my braid. I open our book, keeping it just out of his grasp.

I have been the enchantress, embittered by the needs of pregnant women during a time that I wanted so badly to conceive. I sat through the baby showers, held the newborns, bought the gifts, showed up in early weeks with cookies and flowers. I only relented in my anger after my son arrived safely in the world.

Now I fear that I am both the enchantress and the mother. I look at my tiny son and in my heart I feel love, but I also feel something darker, a love that hurts when it means to protect. I feel the motherly impulse to safeguard him at all costs, which I can only do by locking him away from the world. If I give in to this impulse, my son will grow into a man —strong and safe, but full of resentment and anger — for in keeping him safe, I will have kept him from living.

Sleeping Beauty/La Belle au bois dormant

Il traverse plusieurs chambres pleines de Gentilshommes et de Dames, dormant tous, les uns debout, les autres assis; il entre dans une chambre toute dorée, et il vit sur un lit, dont les rideaux étaient ouverts de tous côtés, le plus beau spectacle qu'il eût jamais vu: une Princesse qui paraissait avoir quinze ou seize ans, et dont l'éclat resplendissant avait quelque chose de lumineux et de divin. Il s'approcha en tremblant et en admirant, et se mit à genoux auprès d'elle. Alors comme la fin de l'enchantement était venue, la Princesse s'éveilla; et la regardant avec des yeux plus tendres qu'une première vue ne semblait le permettre: "Est-ce vous, mon Prince?" lui dit-elle, "vous vous êtes bien fait attendre."

I try to speak to my son in both of my languages interchangeably. I want to believe that he has a preference for French, and each time I read to him in it, the sound of the language soothes him more quickly than the sharper clip of English. I keep a book of Charles Perrault's *Contes* on the nursery bookshelf. Perrault's version of *Sleeping Beauty* is a long one; my mind wanders as I read it, my son looks overhead at his mobile. I occasionally reach up to turn it, keeping him enchanted. My now cold coffee sits on the floor at my feet.

Sleeping Beauty is so docile. She awakens and sees this man kneeling before her and sweetly asks, "Is it you, my prince? You've done so well to wait."

I woke up next to a man I thought I wanted. He was older, a born-and-bred New Yorker who dropped out of his Ph.D. program to write. I was new to the city, a writer who didn't write. He invited me to a dinner party at his house where I met all of his friends. Afterwards, he kissed me and it tasted like bourbon. He slowly unbuttoned all of the minute buttons on the vintage dress I'd chosen because it made my waist look so tiny. In the morning, he took me out for pancakes. I was under a spell that made me think I was lucky he chose me.

In the light of morning, I saw my dress crumpled on the floor. There were no curtains, and the summer sunlight warmed the room. I was sticky from alcohol and sweat. I hoped that my breath wasn't too sour. The man initiated sex but couldn't get it up and asked me to give him a blow job. I acquiesced, but I didn't want to. I was yielding, sweet. When I stopped, he said, "Is that it?" A hint of anger in his voice, a dash of exasperation. Either he was not my prince, or I had failed to be pliant enough.

We rode the train to work in silence and walked into our office together. We didn't speak all day except for when he messaged me to ask if I could translate some copy for him into French.

The Frog Prince

So she picked up the frog with her finger and thumb, carried him upstairs and put him in a corner, and when she had lain down to sleep, he came creeping up, saying: "I am tired and want to sleep as much as you; take me up, or I will tell your father." Then she felt beside herself with rage, and picking him up, she threw the frog with all her strength against the wall, crying: "Now will you be quiet, you horrid frog!"

One of my son's onesies has a pattern of little frogs wearing crowns all over it. "Oh, the frog prince, how cute," I thought when I added it to a cart of baby clothes. As I turn to this fairy tale in our book, I remember that the princess is meant to be the villain. I can't see her that way now. I understand her disgust with the frog who demands to eat from her plate and sleep on her pillow. This frog who already had something in mind when he agreed to fetch her golden ball from the bottom of a well.

My frog prince fooled me for nearly five years. After each kiss, he was still the same critical man, scoffing at my literature degree, belittling my choice in friends. One night, I was taking a bath and looked up from my book and thought, "I don't love him at all." I was the one who transformed when the frog was thrown. I could breathe again.

Little Red Riding Hood

There is a story about another time that Little Red Riding Hood met a wolf on the way to Grandmother's house, while she was bringing her some cakes. The wolf tried to get her to stray from the path, but Little Red Riding Hood was on her guard and kept right on going. She told her grandmother that she had met a wolf and that he had greeted her. But he had looked at her in such an evil way that "If we hadn't been out in the open, he would have gobbled me right up."

I turn on my son's sound machine to the soothing sounds of drying clothes. I'm bored of it. Instead, I change it to wind. It swooshes past us through the room. I open our book to "Little Red Riding Hood." When we get to the classic lines, "But Grandmother, what big eyes you have!" I do it up, exaggerating for comedic effect, and my son giggles and coos in his crib. When I get to the end of the story I know, there is another version printed, one in which Little Red Riding Hood never gets eaten. She senses the danger from the start.

I have met many wolves. They have followed me up and down the platform in a Paris métro station, calling me a *salope*. They have stared at me on the train in New York City and said, "I just want you to know that I'm going to jack off when I think about you later." They have followed me off the train at my stop, scaring me as they trail me around the block. They have been my neighbors, pounding drunkenly on my door, "I know you're in there!" They have disguised themselves as people I loved, only to show their fangs when I got too close. I walk fast through the night now, my keys gripped between my fingers as a weapon.

My son sleeps, his lips puckered. It is my mouth reproduced on his little face. I smooth his hair. "You must never be the wolf," I whisper to him.

Imaginary

I found the letters tucked into an old journal. They fell out along with a sheet of old Photomaton pictures I'd used for my French ID. My eyes are wide, lips unsmiling and painted red, bangs cut crookedly because I used to do it myself with kitchen scissors. Of course I hadn't forgotten R's letters, but I hadn't read them in a long time. They're folded tightly, one of them on the slick paper that he ripped out of our college graduation program, the page indented under his words because he had to bear down so hard with the pen while writing to me through the commencement speech. The other is on notebook paper, written in pencil, faded with time. His handwriting is cramped and scratchy. "I think you're perfect and I'd do or change anything about myself in hopes of consistently making you smile." We were twenty-one.

I had a boyfriend then. I'd been with him all through college; it was expected that we'd get married soon because that's what people do in the South. I didn't love him, but I'd never told R that. Whenever he tried to kiss me, I felt suffocated. I'd push him away and say it must be something in the air, allergies, the medication I'd taken that morning, maybe I was just tired.

When I first read the letters, I sat down on the floor in my nearly empty dorm room and cried. Then I called R and said I'd love it if we could remain friends.

***

I loved my reflection in R's eyes. I felt like a deity at whose feet he worshiped, but when a friend remarks on how often he hovers near me, I say, "It's so sad, isn't it?" with a cruel laugh. Still, I liked him from afar. Once, he was in town and dropped by the bookstore where I worked as a surprise, but I hid in my car. I don't know if I was afraid of him or myself. I told my friends that he was stalking me, but actually I was flattered.

I read all of the books he recommended. I read *The Garden of Eden* by Hemingway, even though I hate Hemingway.

Once when I was house-sitting, I thought about calling him and asking him to come and stay with me. I still had a boyfriend, but I wanted R, or maybe I wanted the me that he thought I was. I did call him, but I didn't ask him to come over. Instead, we talked late into the night. He was sitting outside by his sister's pool, smoking cigarettes—I could hear him inhale and exhale. I knew he rolled the cigarettes himself. I'd watch him do it whenever we'd wait outside the liberal arts building in college. Now I was curled up in a strange bed, my stomach aflutter with guilt and elation.

***

The year I worked in a bookstore, I sometimes flirted with the writers who came in to do book signings. One attractive author once strongly recommended that I read *A Sport and a Pastime,* a flirtation that I didn't understand until I actually read it a year later. I always bragged to R about these encounters. He was a writer, too, and I wanted to make him jealous.

"I aspire to have someone write about me. I'd love to be a muse," I texted him.

"Really? That's pretty self-absorbed of you," he replied.

It stung—I was fishing for him to say that I was already his.

***

We didn't see each other for years. R dated other people. I stayed with the same guy. Online, I'd see the photos of other women with R and I hated them. I loved it when he broke up with them and talked about how annoying they were, though he did feel bad about the girl in Yellowstone whose virginity he took. Part of me was pleased that I'd won out in the battle for his affections, leaving the unhappy girl in Yellowstone, a virgin sacrifice on the altar of me.

***

After graduate school, I came back from France. After years of near constant communication, after finally saying "I love you" over the phone, I changed my flight to come home to him. I was nervous to see him in person, even though I'd been talking to him over Skype for the past year.

We were on opposite schedules then. I woke up early in the morning for class at the Sorbonne and called R on Skype as he'd return from his late-night restaurant shift in New Orleans. Throughout the call, I'd look at the small image of myself in the corner of the screen, applying my makeup, fascinated to see what my own features looked like as I did mundane things. He also looked at me. "You're so beautiful," he'd say, eyes half closing from exhaustion.

I had a layover in Dallas, where I changed clothes and put on makeup. When I landed in New Orleans, I played it cool, like I always did, afraid to show that anything or anyone mattered to me, especially R, who mattered so much. His hands were shaking, and he was sweating. When I hugged him, I felt the warm dampness of the back of his T-shirt.

***

On the page of my journal in which I tucked his letters, I wrote a quote from *Anna Karenina*. The entry is dated three months after I'd come back to Louisiana. I must have been re-reading Anna's story to find some solace in my own unhappiness at being back in the South, bored and unexpectedly lonely.

What I had copied down was from a chapter where Vronsky is hours late to meet Anna:

She placed both hands on his shoulders and gazed at him for a long time with a deep, rapturous, and at the same time, searching look. She studied his face to make up for the time in which she had not seen him.

As at every meeting, she was bringing together her imaginary idea of him (an incomparably better one, impossible in reality) with him as he was.

R was different. He was so angry, sometimes at me, sometimes at the world, but always directed at me because I was there. He slammed doors and complained about his job, his friends, his life. I wondered if I'd somehow created an imaginary idea of him, of us.

He'd moved into an apartment on Iberville Street in New Orleans, and I'd stay weekends with him, expecting us to make up for lost time, but he left me alone for long periods where I lay around on his bed, reading. Once he locked me in the apartment from the outside, saying I shouldn't leave, and then came back to grab some notebooks from on top of the fridge and angrily said, "Just in case you thought you could snoop while you're here." The apartment was mostly bare, no books, clothes crumpled in piles on the floor.

Out of spite, I opened his laptop and read every document saved. None of it was worth anything. Useless fragments of term papers, starts of poems, garbage.

***

My close friends had planned a night out for my birthday. R arrived late, pissed off, forcing me to sit on his lap, too affectionate in front of everyone.

He left early. I went home with my best friend, explaining that he was just stressed, trying to wrap up his thesis while working nights. I didn't want her to see how sad I was, how disappointed, and after all, he was planning to make it up to me tomorrow. He'd gotten a room at a nice hotel downtown.

When we met up the next day, the air between us felt heavy. I felt afraid, though I wasn't sure why. I didn't say anything as I got into the passenger seat of the car and R loaded my suitcase into the back. "I need to stop by Mason's," he said. "I left some medication that I need there."

"Okay," I said, "we haven't seen Mason in a while."

"He's not home. I'm just going in to pick something up."

I went inside and sat down on the couch while R went into the back. I didn't question why he'd left medication at a friend's house. He came back into the living room, livid, yelling about how Mason, his best friend, had stolen his medication.

"Why would your friend steal medicine from you?" I asked, trying to calm him down.

He picked up a pile of books on the coffee table and threw them across the room, so angry that he was close to tears. "Because he's a fucking asshole," he screamed.

I stood there, shocked and repulsed. I didn't mean to, but I started laughing. Then I walked outside to sit on the porch, willing my heartbeat to slow down.

I didn't know R was doing heroin.

***

I kept searching for what I thought must have been the real R—I couldn't understand where the person I'd known and loved had gone. I started to feel crazy, like I'd completely imagined him. The version of myself I'd fallen for, that lovely reflection in his eyes—a woman beautiful, smart, untouchable— she withered and died. I'd become a burden to him instead. He told me, "Don't take this the wrong way, but I have a real life, and things that are bigger than you."

***

The last time I saw R was at his house on Iberville. I came over because he asked me to. I realize now that he was probably scared. He was losing himself, he was so unhappy. I was numb. He stood against the wall and sank down to the floor. It was raining outside, and he was crying. "Please, can't you just love me the way I am?"

As at every meeting, she was bringing together her imaginary idea of him (an incomparably better one, impossible in reality) with him as he was.

Amy

Some friendships rival the intensity of lovers.

***

Amy wasn't my first friend in New York, but whenever I smell her perfume on someone else, it feels like a haunting. I used to get anxious and look around, expecting her to appear next to me, wide smile and beaded septum piercing.

***

I met Amy right after I'd moved to New York. She worked with me at a tech company that touted it was going to "reimagine the world of commerce" with handmade artisan goods. We were both on what they then called the Marketplace Integrity and Trust & Safety teams, MITS for short. We were "MITS girls" to all of the engineers, meaning we were young and hot and barely made any money, and thus, were easily lured by happy hours where all of our drinks would be paid for. I was twenty-four and Amy was twenty-six. I was shy and alone in a city I didn't know. Amy was outgoing and seemed to know everyone. She spoke in hyperbole. Everything was "the best" to her—the sweetest, the most beautiful, the most lovely.

I can summon images of our early days working together—Amy walking in wearing a full fur coat which she draped over the back of her chair (and which one of the office dogs promptly peed on), Amy's long lacquered nails going *click click click clack* on her keyboard while she worked through the hundreds of items we had to review for their "handmade integrity," Amy wearing a skin tight black dress with a pattern of gold chains all over it. "Girl, I know this isn't your style but isn't it so cool? I got it on Fulton Mall."

***

The first time Amy and I ever spent time together outside of the office was when she invited me to something called Presentation Party Night. Her friends put it on every month in Bushwick. It was always on a Sunday and there was always free beer. People gave presentations on any topic imaginable, from the rise of craft beer to cupping. The woman who presented cupping had short dreadlocks and a Marilyn piercing. She stripped a volunteer of his shirt and had him lie face down on a long wooden table. As she explained the medical benefits of cupping, she set a little fire in a glass orb before placing it onto the man's back. It suctioned on, and she did it again and again. I remember the large red welts on his skin as she pulled off the suction cups, each separating from his back with a squelch.

In a photograph taken that night, Amy and I are sitting on the ground in the converted warehouse, both of our heads tilted slightly to the right, as we listen to someone out of frame. Both fair-skinned, my long brown hair cascades down my left shoulder, Amy's vibrant red hair falls over her right. We both look extremely serious. I posted this on Instagram and Amy commented, "Haha, I look deeply suspicious :)".

***

When I came to New York from New Orleans, I was still raw from a breakup with a boyfriend who turned out to be a heroin addict. When Amy came to New York, she was fleeing Minneapolis, where she'd found out her best friend had been fucking her boyfriend. These were stories that we kept close to our hearts, opening up only after several glasses of wine.

***

The tech company where Amy and I met was young and growing when we joined. Nearly everyone who worked there was in their twenties, and because we all spent so much time at work, we were not just coworkers, but friends, lovers, etc. There were no adults there to teach us about work/life balance or boundaries. Everyone knew everyone's business. Feelings were hurt over not receiving particular party invites, over who was sleeping with who.

For me, that was Silas. He was older than me, a native New Yorker, a literature PhD dropout with a penchant for William Faulkner. I was naive enough to take his arrogance for wit. Our time as a couple was relatively short, a few months of disappointing sex and stilted conversations, but our possessiveness of each other lingered. We'd get drunk at work parties and inevitably get into a fight,trying to make each other jealous.

I used Amy as my shield at happy hours and parties. We would huddle together, hold hands, go into the bathroom together. "It makes me happy seeing you two together," Silas remarked to me in a work chat one afternoon. Though we never spoke of it, Amy and I knew that our dynamic was sexy.

***

I got feedback that I should distance myself from Amy. Both the manager and director of our department began to watch us suspiciously, and though I tried to convince Amy otherwise, it became apparent that both women disliked her. She was warned that her work was inadequate. She wasn't answering enough emails, reviewing enough tasks. At the end of the day, we would compare our tally of completed emails and tasks, and they were always nearly the same.

"It's not a good look—it isn't professional the way that you're always with her," the department director told me in a career development session. In my yearly performance review, my manager said, "You do good work, but the other girls on the team don't like you. You and Amy are popular and that can rub people the wrong way. You should rethink that friendship and start socializing with the other girls more."

We stopped sitting together at work, but we communicated via GChats all day. I looked over at Amy's desk where she was hunched over her computer, blinking back tears, typing furiously to hit her quotas. *Click click click clack* went her long fingernails, decadently painted in shiny gold lacquer. I did not make any efforts to build friendships with the other girls.

Once, as we were walking around Fort Greene on a Sunday, Amy turned to me and said, "You know, it's just that they don't like me. I'm different—I stand out! It's offensive to them. You are just what they like. You look the way they want you to, and so they're never going to do this to you. I have this nose ring and I wear big jewelry and you look... classic. I mean, my GOD, I just hate them so much." I stayed quiet while she continued her rant. We reached her apartment in Clinton Hill just as it was getting dark. "Come on mama, let's have a glass of wine, and then I need to do some more work," she sighed, heaving open the heavy wooden door to the three bedroom apartment she shared with five roommates.

***

Amy didn't lose her job, but she unraveled. Now things were the worst, the most hideous, the cruelest. My career grew as hers was snuffed out. I was given new assignments, put in charge of documentation, interviewing for new members of the team, training all of our new hires. I felt defensive when Amy shit-talked our jobs, but I loved her and would listen for hours. Sometimes I'd spend the night in her apartment so we could talk until we fell asleep.

***

There was a party at a vacant apartment in Williamsburg. Amy and I arrived together with beer, sticking to our performance of conjoined twins. The house was decorated haphazardly with streamers, balloons all over the floor, a

DJ set up in one corner of the room. There was, inexplicably, a giant blow-up zebra in the middle of the main room. Silas was there. Ali, his friend, put his arms around the two of us and squeezed us close to him. "Come on you two, it's like we're in an episode of *GIRLS*!"

Silas looked at me, "Do you and Amy want to leave and go get some food?" We followed him out of the house, tipsy, holding hands. "Let's stop in this place for another drink and then we'll find something to eat," he said, leading us into Bushwick Country Club.

I still wanted this man to want me. He went to the bar to order us gin & tonics, and Amy squeezed my arm. "I think this is good, girl. It's good that he's wanting to spend time with you."

The bar was loud; it was impossible to carry a conversation. Amy stepped away and started to dance on the open floor. When I looked to Silas, he had joined her, dancing close to her, his body touching hers. She looked up to the ceiling with her eyes closed and reached her arms above her head gracefully, her body closer to his. I stood still near the wall, gripping my drink. I watched them song after song. Eventually, I walked over and grabbed Amy's arm. She pulled me in between them, moving her hips against mine, but I tugged her arm again. "I want to leave. NOW."

She looked at me, startled. "Okay mama, we'll leave."

We piled into a cab. Amy started chatting with the cab

driver while Silas looked down at his phone. "Where are we going?" I asked him.

"We're going to my house," he said without looking up at me. "I just ordered some food to be delivered there."

"What? I don't want to go to your house. You didn't ask if we wanted to go to your house."

"Kaycie, it's okay," Amy said, turning to me, putting her hand on my arm.

***

Amy commented on how Silas's apartment was the most lovely as she excused herself to the bathroom. He went into his room. I sat down at the kitchen table. Amy came out first, and I looked up at her. "I think you should leave. I want you to leave now," I said quietly.

She looked at me like a startled animal. "Okay, I'll go."

She left without saying anything to Silas, and when he came out of his room, I was sitting alone at the table, drumming my fingernails distractedly. He sat his laptop down on the table.

"Where's Amy?" he said.

"What did you think you were doing? You thought we'd all just sit together here and watch the fucking *Sopranos* on your laptop until maybe you could fuck the two of us?"

He looked down at the floor. I cried on my way home in a cab that I couldn't afford.

***

January 8, 2014 7:50AM

Kaycie: Ugh Amy. I can't sleep anymore and I feel sad. Like can't get out of bed sad

January 8, 2014 10:36AM

Amy: Kaycie, I know. I'm so sorry.

Amy: I don't understand what happened last night. Like, the whole thing was weird

Amy: All of it. Like the dancing and then taking us back to his house. It's all weird

Kaycie: It kind of makes me want to throw up that he was touching you and won't even look at me

Kaycie: In what universe would that ever not hurt me

Amy: He's stupid

Kaycie: It's like oh okay so now I also have to feel insecure about myself in comparison to my only close friend in the city. Okay

Kaycie: Like am I not sexy or funny or interesting enough? Am I annoying?

Amy: Kaycie, don't feel insecure in reference to me. It's not real. He is just dumb and fucked this up. He can't handle anything.

Amy: Do you wanna get brunch and talk?

***

Another work happy hour—Our friend Aaron and his girlfriend Nicole discussed Aaron's upcoming birthday party.

"He has two lists," Nicole said. "It's ridiculous. One list is the shortlist in case I choose a smaller venue, and one list is the long list in case I pick a bigger bar."

"Hey, it matters. If it's a small get-together, I need to have only the important people there," Aaron smirked.

"Oh my god, are you serious?" Amy giggled. "Can we see the lists? I want to see them."

"Yeah, show them to us," I chimed in.

Nicole showed us her phone. My name was on the shortlist, but Amy's was not.

"Oh, I see how it is," she said, "I'm not as important as Kaycie, okay." She smiled.

The next morning I was sitting in my sparsely furnished apartment in Bed-Stuy, huddled on my couch and nursing a cup of coffee. My laptop was perched on the heavy antique coffee table that Amy had helped me load into an Uber and carry up two flights of stairs last year. A GChat popped up from Amy.

Feb 13, 2014 7:21AM

Amy: Do you think i should feel dumb about Aaron?

Amy: I feel dumb.

Amy: And I feel dumb for feeling dumb.

Kaycie: Wait why?

Amy: like this stupid party thing.

Amy: i feel so dumb

Kaycie: you shouldn't feel anything about it.

Kaycie: it doesn't mean anything, you were invited.

Kaycie: Aaron and I have just hung out a few more times, and he knows me from the context of Bonnie and Silas and other parties, so he's just interacted with me a few more times. It doesn't mean anything.

Amy: yes ok

Kaycie: don't be upset about that. He's dumb for doing that.

Kaycie: also I will BOYCOTT his birthday for hurting your feelings. THAT IS NOT ALLOWED.

Amy: awww i love you

Amy: i'm just, so so so sensitive and hurt about work that like one leeeetle thing that echoes it outside of work just destroys me

Amy: so, i'll work on it and stop being a baby

Kaycie: Aw Amy I understand. I don't think anyone thinks more of me than they do of you. I really don't

Amy: I was thinking like

Amy: I've always been best friends with people (ok, this is gonna sound shitty but let me say it)- I've always been best friends with people that are more beautiful and more successful than I am

Amy: part of me was thinking, I mean, I could just make friends that are less pretty and successful than me lol

Amy: BUT I DON'T WANT TO

Amy: so I just have to tell myself that, the reason my beautiful and successful best friends want me as a friend is because I am interesting and I do have something to offer

Kaycie: I understand. Amy I have always always felt that way too

Kaycie: Like I'm the quiet less pretty less desirable friend

Kaycie: I always felt that way

Kaycie: But you are not less beautiful or successful

Kaycie: No one loves me more than they do you. They just don't

***

Another work party—this time in the Lower East Side. Our company's head security engineer was leaving, and they had an open tab. I arrived first, flitting around from person to person until Amy arrived. At some point, Amy had struck up a conversation with Ali and then the three of us were in the back of an Uber, heading to a dance party in Williamsburg. "I have molly," Ali said. "Good stuff. Do you want some?"

Amy and I looked at each other. "Dude, let's do it," she said. We turned to Ali with our hands out.

My mind was void of thought, there was only a warm happiness. Amy pulled me onto the stage with the DJ, and we danced. She pulled me close to her, her lips on mine, and I let her, kissing her back, eyes closed. I loved her, of course I did, I loved everyone. Ali pulled me into his arms, but Amy shoved him away. "No, you can't have her. Don't touch her."

We migrated to someone's apartment, where Amy and I spent most of the time in the bathroom, exclaiming how large our pupils are. "We look so crazy," I laughed.

"You look just like a doll, you have, like, doll eyes," Amy said, as we stood shoulder to shoulder, each of us staring at the other's reflection.

The next day I woke up in my own bed, Amy next to me, her mascara smeared. "That was so much fun," she said, grinning. The molly hadn't worn off yet. We walked from Bed-Stuy to Clinton Hill, hand in hand, marveling at how we felt, and startling the barista when we ordered cappuccinos, our pupils as big as buttons when we told him we'd both take the same thing.

***

My career continued to grow. I created a new position for myself, got a raise and started reporting to the director of our department. Amy's career stalled. We sat eating eggs benedict at a mediocre brunch spot between our two apartments. "I spent three hours on Saturday just closing out tasks and then two more hours working on documentation for training," she said, barely touching her food, grasping her coffee mug in both hands. "It just doesn't even matter what I do. They don't like me, so I can do more work than you and it will never even matter."

I was quiet, shoveling food into my mouth because I wanted this brunch to be over.

***

Amy got a new job. I cried on her last day when she walked out of the door without me, waving goodbye to our team.

She threw herself a goodbye party in the backyard of her Clinton Hill apartment. She invited all of our work friends, strung up fairy lights. There was a grill, plenty of beer and wine. Halfway through the evening, Silas showed up, a dimwitted undergrad on his arm. "What is he doing here? Did you invite him?" I hissed at Amy.

"Yeah, girl, it's chill, I mean, I'm friends with him."

I spent the rest of the evening complaining to another

friend about how inconsiderate she was to invite him, how rude of him to show up to my closest friend's party.

The next day we drank beers at 11am, followed by large iced coffees. We made ourselves nauseated. We sat on a stranger's stoop, leaning back against the steps, lazy in the heavy summer air. I took a few photos of us on my phone. I had cut my hair short, just above my shoulders, and I was wearing big sunglasses. Amy's long red hair was pulled into a messy topknot, and she was wearing a turquoise bubble necklace, which I hated for being so ostentatious.

"So, I didn't tell you this last night because I didn't want to hurt your feelings, but my sister caught Silas making out with that girl on our couch. Like, really going for it."

I looked at her. "So then why are you telling me now?"

***

We spoke less and less often. I stopped walking over to her apartment. One day, Amy sent me a long text asking for distance because she couldn't have my toxicity in her life at this moment. I never answered it. Instead, I took a screenshot and sent it to another friend who replied, "Were you two dating? Is she breaking up with you?"

***

Years passed. I started dating the man I would eventually marry. I took a new job—a big corporate one with a livable salary and actual adults for coworkers.

***

In Grand Central, I walked past a woman and smelled Amy's perfume. I remembered our "secret place" in the East Village where we both always ordered a gin cocktail that the waitress would bring out and then, to our delight, gently spray with rosewater. I don't remember the name of the place and doubt I could find it again by myself. We had vowed to never take anyone else there.

***

I got married. I invited Amy. She brought her handsome boyfriend and her little rescue dog. They arrived at 11pm the night before the ceremony. I was sitting with a group of friends when I saw her through the window. I jumped up to greet her. She hugged me tightly. "Oh, I love you so much, this is perfect. Just come out here and be with me for a minute," she said, lighting a cigarette.

"I love you too," I replied, taking a drag.

***

On the day of the wedding, I watched from my window as our guests arrived. At the corner of the parking lot, I saw Amy, the sun shining on her vibrant red hair. She wasn't looking at her phone or watching the other guests. All alone, she stood quietly, looking down at the ground, smoking her skinny Turkish cigarette, wrapped in a heavy black coat.

Too Complicated

When I was thirty-one, I decided to stop taking antidepressants. I decided this because I'd gotten fatter. Since I was working out excessively and dieting constantly, people told me it was the Lexapro. I figured I'd been fine enough for awhile, so early in the year, I found a new psychiatrist. I told him I was ready to quit.

His office reminded me of a cheap apartment you'd find in a college town—brown carpet and eggshell walls that looked like they could have been made of cardboard. His bookshelf seemed mostly to be a display case for those glass paperweights with bursts of color inside of them. I'd always wondered who bought those. It made me wonder if he'd somehow given someone the impression that he liked these and thus had been gifted one every year.

He was old and bald and Irish, maybe not that old, but the lack of hair made it hard to tell. He was reading my intake questions while I sat quietly in front of him.

"Do you ever have thoughts of suicide?" he asked.

"Sometimes I think about what it would be like to not exist, but I don't imagine myself committing suicide."

"That's too complicated, too much to write," he replied.

Before I could think too hard on a shrink calling the questioning of my own existence too complicated, he started rattling off instructions.

"Are you going to write this down? I don't think you'll remember it, so write it down."

2 weeks on 5mg
2 weeks every other day on 5mg, tempered with Wellbutrin

"Once you get off of this, you'll see. Whatever weight you've gained will just melt right off," were, I believe, my psychiatrist's exact words.

I followed these directives dutifully. One thing he hadn't bothered to tell me about was the withdrawal.

Four weeks later, waves of nausea rolled over me every afternoon as I'd sit at my desk and silently will no one to approach me. Partially because I didn't think I could speak, but also because I had lost the ability to stop myself from crying. It eventually dawned on me that my brain was punishing me for taking away the little white pills.

The worst part is what they call "brain zaps." I had never experienced anything like these before and had to do my own research to find out what they were called. They are apparently "uncaused sensations of electricity briefly passing through the brain." They felt like hot bright flashes and then dizziness, nausea, crying. It got so bad that I had to tell my boss I was going through some "medical stuff," as I was quite certain that he'd noticed me blinking back tears at my desk.

Unsure of whether this was normal, I called my psychiatrist, the paperweight enthusiast.

"Hi? Hey yeah, I've been feeling really bad since quitting my antidepressants. Like anxious and sick—nauseated, dizzy. Is this normal? Is there something I can do to make it stop?"

"Please hold," the receptionist said.

Ten minutes passed. I paced near my office window, twelve floors up, looking down at the ant-sized humans scurrying around Park Avenue.

"The doctor said it's normal. We'll see you again at your next appointment." *Click.*

I thought I could handle just another week or two of feeling unwell. What I didn't realize was that the depression I thought I'd successfully beaten had woken up and started manifesting itself again, settling comfortably back into my every thought. When I picture it now, I see an animated movie where a poisonous gas creeps slowly across the technicolor landscape, weaving its way into homes, across forests, wilting all of the plants in its path while the protagonist plods along blissfully unaware of the danger sneaking in.

To my credit, it wasn't so noticeable at first. Once the physical symptoms eased, I spent my mornings in a manic state, which I enjoyed. I didn't think I was manic. What I thought was *wow how great! I guess it's true that I didn't even need those anymore!* I was chatty with friends, texting everyone I knew as I got ready in the mornings. I had so much to say! I was chatty with strangers on the train, complimenting them and basking in that warm fuzzy feeling of being a nice person. I found so much meaning in everything—everything I read during that period is highlighted, underlined, scribbled in the margins. Everything felt so bright.

But the poisonous gas kept creeping in, and soon I started to worry every time I left the house, convinced I'd left a burner on, left a candle lit, didn't lock the door. My head became foggy. I started doing senseless things—walking into the street without looking, missing my subway stop.

One night, I sat in the bathroom painting my nails. I dropped a glass bottle of clear polish and watched it shatter at my feet. I immediately reached down to sweep the mess up with my hands, the pain not registering for a few seconds as I looked blankly down at my palms, sparkling with polish and tiny embedded pieces of glass, drops of red beginning to drop onto the spill.

The sadness came after the fog; it swallowed me up. I stopped texting my friends in the mornings, I stopped helping strangers, stopped complimenting them on the train. Everything felt like a slog. My body felt heavy.

My anxiety about leaving the house morphed into a fear of leaving the house. I was afraid something bad was a certainty if I left. I didn't know what it would be, but I felt I could protect myself and others from it if I didn't leave home. I couldn't explain to anyone why I didn't want to leave. There was a crushing weight on my chest, paralyzing me from making any decisions. I became irritated with other people for no reason—annoyed that anyone would try to get my attention, would try to make me laugh, would try to ask my advice, would dare to ask me how I was doing. *I'm fine.* So I stayed in my apartment on my days off, laying on the couch, staring up at the ceiling, my dog trying to rouse me with cries and pushing his head into my hand for pets.

A trip I'd planned with my best friend, my bachelorette trip, arrived. One week in the French Riviera followed by three days in Paris, the place I'd been happiest in my life. I was afraid to go.

"Why are you being like this?" my fiancé asked. "You love France. You love Meryl. It's going to be great. What's wrong?"

"I don't know," I said, curling into myself on the couch, tears welling up.

In France, I berated myself in my head. *You're fat, you're lazy. You'll look back at this trip and see in the photos how fat and lazy you are, how thin and perfect your friend is.* I laid on the beach in the French Riviera, a dream vacation, two halves of my brain fighting each other. One half hating myself, telling me that I didn't deserve to exist, how could I let myself order pasta for lunch, the other half begging me to stop because why would I waste this trip? I anxiously smoked so many cigarettes that I made myself nauseated, and then I'd resolve to put an end to all of this, to enjoy myself, but the next day I'd just do it all again.

The first time I thought about suicide I was in a spin class that I'd dragged myself to during my lunch hour. I'd started to become afraid of going to the gym, afraid of spending my lunch away from my desk. If I'd made it out of my apartment that day, my desk became the place I couldn't leave. It had been excruciating to get myself into this gym, a mere two blocks away from my office. I sat on my stationary bike as the instructor was helping other people set up. Fiddling with my watch I felt the overwhelming urge to no longer feel. Not necessarily to die but to just. . . not be. It was such a calm, matter of fact thought. *What if I just opted out? It would be so calm, so quiet, so. . . nothing.* Then I laughed, what a stupid place to think these thoughts, in this overpriced gym in midtown Manhattan where all of these businessmen are asking for help adjusting their bikes that go nowhere. Besides, the other half of my brain protested. I needed to work hard in this class so I could stop being fat and lazy, so I'd be good enough to live a good life, to get married, to have a kid.

Three more months passed, then four, and none of the weight came off. In addition to believing I was fat, I started to worry about my hair, panicking every time I showered and a few strands came out in my hands. I became obsessed with my appearance, with telling myself how disgusting I was. I just needed to be better, work harder, will my body and mind to comply.

Part of me knew that I was sick, that I wasn't taking care of myself, but part of me felt that to go back to the pills would be to fail.

My fiancé and I had plans to meet up for drinks with a friend, the officiant for our wedding. We were supposed to have a cheerful discussion about what we wanted our ceremony to be like. We were getting married in a month.

I'd stayed home from work that day because I'd woken up and felt that I couldn't leave the apartment, laying still in bed, willing my chest to feel less heavy. There was an exercise I read about online where you should just lie there and say aloud to yourself three things that you see in front of you, then three sounds you could hear, and finally you were supposed to slowly move your fingers and toes.

Brick wall. White blanket. Lamp. Fan. Neighbor's music. Cars.

It was supposed to center you and bring your thoughts back to the present. I did it over and over again, but I guess I wasn't doing it right.

Because we'd already made these plans to meet with our friend, and there was a certain amount of normalcy that I wanted to maintain, I put on makeup, took a deep breath, and went into the city.

I arrived too early. I wandered aimlessly around NoLita until five minutes before I was supposed to be at the bar. My fiancé had arrived before me. I pulled up the seat next to him and ordered an Aperol spritz. This bar never properly mixed spritzes. I reached for one of the rolls of silverware set out for dinner and took out the butter knife.

"Did you know it's bad luck to stir things with a knife?" I asked my fiancé, as I lazily mixed my drink.

"No, I've never heard that before," he said. "Are you okay?"

"Richard's nearly here. He just had some train issues," I said, glancing down at my phone, evading the question.

We sat and discussed the MTA, Jewish wedding ceremony details, and whether or not we wanted a poem to be read as part of our vows. I clutched my drink, willed myself to laugh when appropriate, and otherwise let the conversation lunge forward without me. I felt on the verge of tears, teetering on the barstool, and I felt that my performative normalcy wasn't working. I was interacting with the world too stiffly, like an automaton in red lipstick, but it was the best I could do.

When our friend left, my fiancé asked me again how I was doing, and I hesitated to say. We had a month until our wedding. How I was doing was that I was disgusting and miserable and didn't want people to look at me on my wedding day and see that. I didn't want to say that out loud, though, so I said I was tired and I'd had a tough day.

We stood waiting for the train in the Bowery station. I watched the lights of the approaching J train, and for the briefest moment, I thought about Anna Karenina throwing herself into the tracks. I wasn't going to do it, but still, I felt ashamed, and my shield of normalcy caved in on itself for the night. I didn't talk to my fiancé the rest of the way home, irritating him, because he thought I was holding on to some small grudge or comment that I wasn't going to explain.

I didn't want to die. I just wanted my brain to shut up, to stop the poison from filling it, to stop spewing vitriol at myself. I didn't want to wake up in the morning and wander around my apartment, unable to read, unable to go outside, unable to even choose a TV show. I wanted to be unafraid to leave the house, to be able to sit down and read a book without my mind racing.

Whenever my fiancé would ask me if I was thinking about killing myself, I'd get angry. No, why would you think that? I'd tell my therapist *I can't believe David thinks I would kill myself.* But of course, we all lie to our therapists.

That October, my fiancé went away for a long weekend with friends, his bachelor party. Normally thrilled to have the apartment to myself for any amount of time, I was afraid that I'd somehow destroy our life while he was away—by leaving the oven on, forgetting to lock the door, not properly harnessing our dog to the leash before a walk. I couldn't trust my own brain to follow through with the most basic tasks, and now there would be no one to check behind me if I made a mistake. To ensure I didn't fuck things up, I spent the weekend inside, drinking bottles of wine to fall asleep, my dog in the same room at all times. I checked the burners and the oven compulsively before bed. I flipped the deadbolt back and forth to ensure it was really sticking. And when I'd gotten into bed, I'd get up one more time and check it all again.

My fiancé came home on a Monday. At my wit's end, nerves frayed, I'd taken a sick day and laid on the couch all day. I ordered Indian takeout for our dinner and sat quietly huddled into the corner of the couch, staring ahead while my fiancé recalled his trip. While trying to make a noise to indicate my interest in his story, my face betrayed me, and I let out a sob over a bowl of chicken korma. I'd been nervously shredding naan into tiny pieces as he was talking, finally revealing that I'd been quietly allowing myself to disintegrate.

That Wednesday, I returned to the psychiatrist. He'd gotten a new painting for his waiting room. It covered nearly an entire wall, a crudely rendered horse reared up on his hind legs. Its eyes were red and wild, and it looked to me like a demon horse situated in hell, the sky behind him red and orange. Painted above him was the word MUSTANG. I wonder how many patients had nightmares about this painting after staring at it, waiting for their medications to be refilled.

Miscarrying

I stepped outside the medical plaza and texted my husband. *The baby is dying. I'm going to miscarry again.* He was several blocks away, running an errand. I saw him running towards me from far off, a speck getting closer and closer, his face obscured by a black mask, just like mine. I just stood there.

March

The first one was what they call a "chemical pregnancy," which just means it was so early on that they'd never seen the baby on an ultrasound, so early that it was probably just the size of a poppy seed, too small to try to look at. Doctors don't really count these as miscarriages because they happen so early that often women haven't yet realized that they're pregnant, but all I know is that I was pregnant and then I wasn't.

My husband and I, having just married in November, were getting ready to go on our honeymoon, a two-week trip to Japan, when we found out. "I guess I can't have any sushi, but I'm willing to live with that," I said, happy to make the not insignificant sacrifice.

In the office, my coworkers crowded around a computer, looking at a map from Johns Hopkins that was charting the spread of a new disease. On the screen, little red clusters of the virus popped up in Japan from a cruise ship. We cancelled our honeymoon. We'd schedule a babymoon instead, later that summer, when everything calmed down. Maybe we'd go to the south of France.

I read Rivka Galchen's *Little Labors* and thought about how I would one day write about the little being growing inside of me. Sometimes I tried reading aloud to the baby, which according to an app that I downloaded to track the growth by French pastry size, was technically called a blastocyst at this point. But there are no French pastries as small as a blastocyst, so the app said it was the size of a fleur de sel, a tiny flake of sea salt on top of a caramel.

A week later, I woke up to find clumps of dark red blood in my underwear. "David, David, I lost it. I lost the baby," I cried from the bathroom. When I came out, he tried to pull me back into bed to comfort me. "Wait, stop," I said, stripping off the bloody underwear and leggings. I didn't want to bleed all over our white sheets.

I took some time off from work, a recovery gift to myself—time to rest, go to museums, take long walks. Instead, I ended up laying on the couch, barely leaving the house. We stopped taking the subway when the virus finally arrived in the city, so that limited my movement, but mostly I was depressed. My mind replayed the shock of the dark red clots in my underwear. I didn't realize these days that I spent laying on the couch were my last precious moments of actually being able to leave the house.

By the end of my staycation, New York closed down because of the virus. I ventured out only for a few appointments to make sure that the miscarriage was complete. We still felt safe taking cabs then. We thought only the subway was dangerous. Cabs were probably okay. We were lucky to have hand sanitizer, a hot commodity now. Get in the car, buckle your seatbelt, furiously rub your hands with sanitizer. If we forgot to buckle our seatbelts before putting on the hand sanitizer, we'd have to take the hand sanitizer out again and furiously scrub our hands once more.

I was determined to get pregnant again. This lockdown couldn't last more than a month, maybe two. I hoped to re-emerge from this whole ordeal pregnant once again. I googled and convinced myself that it was unlikely that I'd miscarry twice in a row. This next one would be okay. Getting pregnant again became my only goal. I needed to achieve just this one thing during lockdown.

April

I was able to fall pregnant again almost immediately. "Fall pregnant" is what British people say instead of "get pregnant." I'd learned that in the mommy forums I read. Through the rest of March I laid awake for hours after my husband had fallen asleep, my phone lighting up my face, alternating between news stories about the coronavirus and mommy forum posts from 2010 about strangers who'd miscarried and then gone on to have a healthy baby. I couldn't believe my luck when I took a test and saw a faint blue line signaling a positive. I took four more tests, spaced out, just to be sure. I kept two of them on my dresser for weeks to remind myself that I'd accomplished my goal.

Now came the challenge of how to get to a doctor's appointment while a new plague was surging around us. We lived in Bushwick, much too far to walk to an appointment in Bay Ridge. I read articles about Uber drivers being infected, infected people getting in cabs. Were the germs just floating around in the air? Hundreds of people were dying every day in NYC alone. It didn't seem like hand sanitizer would be enough anymore.

My in-laws live in Coney Island. "They have two cars, don't they? Let's just ask to borrow one for the appointment," I said. An easy solution. My father-in-law had a company car that he was still driving around the city because, for some reason, as a manager of a car wash chain, he'd been deemed an essential worker. "Since it's early, I don't want to tell them that I'm pregnant, " I said, "so try telling them that I need to get to the doctor, that I need to have bloodwork done for my thyroid." This was true. I have an autoimmune disease, a worry for a healthy pregnancy.

When my father-in-law next called, my husband and I were both sitting on the couch. I was mindlessly playing *Animal Crossing*. It had become the one thing that I found relaxing. I loved walking around my island, ripping up weeds, digging up fossils, and collecting bugs for a museum run by an owl. My husband and his family are loud talkers, so I overheard the entire conversation over the calming music of my virtual island, where my avatar was toddling around planting flowers and shaking trees to collect branches.

“Hey Dad, so I need to ask you for something. Would it be possible for us to borrow the other car? Kaycie needs to have some bloodwork done for her thyroid,” my husband explained.

A pause.

“You’re not on my insurance,” my father-in-law replied. “Can’t you just put her in an Uber?”

My husband was quiet, but his father kept talking.

“It’s crazy what’s happening, but I’m just glad that you and your sister are okay. Your sister and my two granddaughters. Yeah, I’m just grateful you’re all safe, and that’s all that matters.”

Next to my husband, I started to cry.

“Hey Dad, listen. Actually, Kaycie is pregnant. We need to get to a doctor. Don’t tell anyone okay? We don’t want to tell anyone because it’s early, but I really need the car.”

Another pause.

“Oh wow, Mazel Tov! Tell Kaycie I said congratulations. Have you told your mother? Why don’t you talk to your mother? I’m sorry, David, you’re just not on the insurance.”

I was used to snide comments, interruptions every time I tried to speak up at family dinners, the death by a thousand papercuts approach from my in-laws, but I was not prepared for the ache that came with realizing how little my life meant to them, how little the life of my unborn child meant. Now I could quantify it.

My mother-in-law called later that same evening, indignant that she hadn't been told first about my pregnancy. My husband took the call into another room, but I heard him from down the hall. "Mom, I'm going to stop you right there. No, Mom, we didn't want to tell anyone about it yet, but we felt like we had to because we need to borrow the car." A long pause and then his voice got louder. My dog, sitting on my lap, was suddenly alert. "Do you want to know why my wife feels like none of you love her? Because your car insurance is more important than her safety, that's why."

I told my husband that I would never let them see our child. At night, when he fell asleep, I cried, googling, "Why do my in-laws not like me." I was angry that my husband didn't do more to punish them, to hurt them back. "They're my family, Kaycie," he would say, "what else do you want me to do?" "Well," I replied, "your father is either incredibly fucking stupid or he has no empathy." "I feel like you're saying that my parents don't love me," he replied quietly. I don't envy him, caught between his wife and his parents, and so I backed down. "I'm sure they love you," I sighed, but what I thought was *maybe they don't*. When they later called me, curious about how my first appointment went, the appointment for which they would not let us have use of their spare car, I didn't pick up or call back.

When I told my best friend that I was pregnant, she drove over and delivered a care package—lavender belly oil and Epsom salts, non-alcoholic beer, chocolates. She buzzed into our building and dropped the package in front of our apartment door. I held my dog at the window and waved at her when she went back onto the street. She looked up at us, waving so furiously that the bandana she'd tied around her face in lieu of a mask fell off. I didn't mean to, but I started to cry. It was strange seeing her that way; from all that we'd been told about the virus, it seemed like a real possibility that we would hurt each other if we hugged. An invisible enemy waited to be breathed out, to send someone we loved to the hospital. I shifted my dog onto my hip and waved his paw at her as she stood in the street, still furiously waving up at us. My husband was in the kitchen meticulously wiping down every item from the care package with rubbing alcohol.

In the end, it was my best friend who offered up her car for my doctor's appointments. For each appointment, my husband would bike forty minutes across Brooklyn to her house, leave his bike inside of her building, wipe down the car with Clorox wipes, drive to pick me up, take me to the doctor, wander around Bay Ridge for the duration of my appointment, drive me home, drive the car back, and then bike another forty minutes back to our apartment in Bushwick. I was anxious each time he made the journey back and forth. I clutched my phone, watching his little dot move across the screen on Find My Friends.

For the second time in my life, I stopped taking antidepressants in preparation of getting pregnant. I only wanted one child, one pregnancy, and I was willing to grit my teeth and bear it, willing to eradicate all possible risks. But I had not anticipated a miscarriage or a pandemic. Some days, I barely managed to get out of bed. I set up parental controls on my own phone so I'd stop scrolling through Twitter and refreshing the news to read about death.

At seven weeks into my pregnancy, I gagged at the smell of my husband's morning coffee. Nearly all food was turning my stomach. I felt like my joints were too loose, like if I moved my legs too much they would pop right out of their sockets. I was getting shooting pains in my boobs as they swelled, making all of my bras feel like corsets. My general practitioner told me not to exercise except for light yoga and walking, but I was too afraid to go for walks, and yoga seemed like a surefire way to pop my legs out of their loose sockets. I rubbed my stomach, trying to pick myself up for the little life inside, but sometimes the best I could manage was just to get out of bed to sit on the couch for a few hours.

For my first prenatal appointment, I was masked and wearing the only gloves I had, little grey knit winter gloves. I ordered disposable ones online, but they were all backordered and wouldn't arrive until late May. I was alone, my husband forbidden to come inside with me. I'd never seen this doctor before, but I was referred by my GP who wanted me to see a doctor as soon as possible. The doctor I wanted to work with wouldn't see me until I was at least ten weeks. They were cutting down on the prenatal care they offered due to the virus. I was too early for this first appointment, frowned upon because waiting rooms weren't supposed to exist in the time of virus.

It was hard to fill out my intake paperwork with the knit gloves on and impossible to get into my phone for my pharmacy information. I eventually took one off, glancing up at the front desk, afraid I might get yelled at for allowing my hand to be naked for even a moment. The waiting room was not notable except for a glass display case. I took a photo of it, thinking I'd show it to my kid one day. "Look at this weird thing I looked at so many times when I was pregnant with you."

A little babushka did my intake. She ran a thermometer over my forehead and showed me the temperature. "Is normal, yes?" And then "you want to keep the baby?" She was wearing scrubs patterned with little cartoon cats, and I complimented them while she was drawing my blood. She was suddenly animated, telling me about how much she loved her pet cat. She asked if I had one, and I said, "No, my husband is allergic. My small dog sometimes acts like a cat though." She shook her head in disappointment.

She must have been in her sixties at least. She was risking her life to be here at work, taking my temperature and drawing my blood. From what I'd read, it seemed you were pretty much a goner if the virus caught you over fifty five. Yet here she was, drawing the blood of a stranger, while I'd been terrified just to get into my best friend's car.

I was instructed to go into an examination room and wait, naked from the waist down. When the sonographer came in, she didn't speak much as she squirted jelly onto my stomach, running her wand over it. Eventually, she told me to open my legs wider and then stuck the wand up there too. I looked at the black and white blobs on the screen, but I had no idea what I was looking for. Finally, she explained to me that she saw the fetus and the sac. She told me how many inches it was. "I'm seven and a half weeks along. Is that how big it's supposed to be?" I asked. "We don't know when you got pregnant exactly since you didn't have a period between your last pregnancy, so I can't tell you that. It looks like you're probably about six and a half weeks along though." I didn't argue with her, but I didn't see how that was possible.

When the doctor came in, she told me that there was no heartbeat yet, but she didn't seem worried. I'd need to come back next week to see if the heartbeat had started. "So, do you want to talk about food and exercise now or wait until next week?" she asked. She had a hint of a Russian accent. "I guess now is fine," I replied, pulling a note up on my phone. "I actually have a list of questions prepared." A twinge of worry sprouted in the back of my mind at the mention of only measuring six weeks pregnant, but I held a little ultrasound picture, and I was excited. I wanted to do everything right.

All of my questions answered, I walked back to the car with my husband, clutching the little photo of our fetal pole. This one had made it past being a blastocyst. The app told me that it was the size of a lavender bud. I could still barely tell what I was looking at in the black and white blobs of the ultrasound printout, but it seemed plausible that it was lavender bud sized. I sent the photo to my best friend. "Look, there's my baby!" I tried to feel a sense of relief that the doctor had seen it on the screen. Deep down though, I didn't believe that I was only six weeks along. That would mean that I'd gotten my first positive pregnancy test at only three weeks pregnant.

"I'm worried about them not finding a heartbeat," I told my husband, my best friend, the Google search bar, "but it seems like this can happen sometimes, I guess." Google gave me lots of mommy blogs and forums filled with stories about people who found their baby's heartbeats in the seventh week, eighth week, second appointments. This could be normal, I told myself, trying to steady my own heartbeat.

May

Again, I went upstairs alone, masked and wearing my little grey knit gloves. My temperature was taken. First room on the right, take off everything from the waist down. I climbed onto the chair, pulled the little pink paper robe over myself, nervously trying to be modest even though these people were literally about to have me spread my legs while they shoved a sonogram stick up my vagina.

The ultrasound technician came in, re-entered my info, shoved the stick up there. She waved it around, clicking on the screen. *Click click. Click click.* I gasped from a sudden sharp pain. "Oh sorry," she said, continuing to press down, "it seems like you have a gas bubble here so that's going to be painful, but I need to take more measurements." *Click, click.* Then she went to the door and opened it slightly "Dr. A. Dr. A!" When the doctor didn't appear, she tried to be light, smiling, she said, "She never hears me. I'll be right back." Sitting there, half naked, clutching that pink paper covering, I knew. My heart beat faster and faster, and then it slowed because, deep down, I wasn't surprised. This one, my second one, wasn't okay, was dead, would be dead.

The doctor rushed in and the ultrasound technician shoved the stick back inside of me, moved it around, *click click, click click,* they were both silent. She hit a button, and I heard thumping and rushing sounds.

After several long moments of silence, my doctor spoke. "So, the baby hasn't grown since last week, and at this point, we'd expect to see some growth. It was this length last week, and it remains the same. There is a heartbeat now, but it is much slower than we would expect at this point," she said, not unkindly. "It will likely be a miscarriage." The ultrasound technician pulled her wand out of me and quietly left the room. I saw her take the printed ultrasound photo and place it quietly in the garbage. I sat there, trying not to cry, feeling undignified because I was still half naked and covered in ultrasound jelly. A few days ago my app changed to say that my baby was now the size of a berlingot candy. "Oh I see," I finally managed to say.

"Have you had any spotting?" the doctor asked. "No, I haven't," I said. "Is it normal… for there to be a heartbeat now if it's not. . . going to make it?" I asked. "Well," she said, "it's slower than we would expect. It's possible that the heartbeat started soon after we saw you last week and now it's slowing down, getting ready to stop. If this had been your first appointment with us, I would think it was probably fine, but because we saw you last week, and I have a data point…I'm sorry. We can have you come back in one week or two weeks to see what happens. Which would you prefer?"

"One week," I said, blinking back tears in front of this stranger, a kind stranger, but still a stranger, "I don't want to drag it out longer than I have to."

I didn't think to ask anything about what my options were. I was alone, and I was half naked, and I was trying not to cry in front of people I barely knew, so I ended the conversation and calmly scheduled my follow-up appointment in one week.

Very few people witnessed my husband running to me, gathering me in his arms, and the two of us masked, crying in the street. "Why though," I cried, trying not to crumple onto the ground. I was crying, but in the moment it felt like I was faking it. I felt empty, a woman guilty of losing two children, a woman foolish enough to think she could outrun a year of death by giving new life in a world stricken with disease.

At home, my husband asked me lots of questions that I didn't have the answers to. I refused to call the office. My husband called the doctor back himself, while I signed into a virtual therapy session. "My baby is going to die," I told my therapist when he logged on. "They said to come back in a week, but probably it's going to die."

Every week since early March had felt long, but this one was the longest. I was either staring at my phone or pacing back and forth in my apartment while listening to Cuomo give me the daily death tolls. We didn't know whether or not we were at the apex yet. Each day, I announced the deaths to my husband, optimistic at the decrease from nearly 800 a day. The ultrasound photo was taken down from our fridge. My husband didn't say anything or tell me what happened to it, but I was thankful to see that it was gone.

During that week of waiting, I would sometimes do something that resembled praying even though I don't believe in a god. *If there's something out there, please please keep my baby alive. Let my baby be alive and let it catch up and the heartbeat speed up. Please.*

When the time came for me to return to that drab little medical plaza in Bay Ridge, I steeled myself mentally. I complimented the ultrasound technician's haircut. She'd chopped her long straight hair to just below the shoulders and added bangs. I wondered if she had a hairstylist friend because it looked good, styled. We weren't allowed to get haircuts. It seemed especially likely that the virus might get you in a salon, all of those people so close to your face. I'd been hacking at my own bangs by myself with kitchen scissors every time they got so long I had to part them away from my eyes. They were lopsided.

"It's okay," I said to the technician as she moved the sonogram wand around, "I'm prepared this time." "I'm so sorry," she said. "I really am sorry." "It's okay," I said, overcompensating with my cheerful tone. No growth and the heartbeat was gone. It felt like a double failure that my body still hadn't registered that this thing it was fighting so hard to protect and grow was already dead. I hadn't had any spotting, no bleeding at all. I was still swallowing back bouts of nausea, subsisting on saltines and Starbursts. My boobs were sore, preparing to make milk that no one needed.

Because of the coronavirus, the D&C process was not available to me. I would need to be put under for that, and for now, I was not allowed to go into a hospital because there was no room for me there. I could wait to see if my body would expel the pregnancy on its own, but that could take up to six weeks, so the only real option was to take the medication, what I guess some people would call "abortion pills." They're little pills that you push up your vagina, they absorb into your bloodstream, and then your body reacts by contracting until the baby is pushed out.

I hurriedly typed instructions into my Notes app while talking to the doctor:

Take 500-800 mg ibuprofen before using the medication and then every six hours as long as you're cramping. Lay down on the bed and put in four tablets as far as they go, stay in bed for twenty minutes. If they fall out after twenty minutes, that's fine. One to four hours after, expect cramping and bleeding, should be heavy bleeding. That can last for hours and then gets better. If nothing happens, wait until Sunday and then call again.

It was Tuesday, and the doctor recommended that I do this on Saturday because I would not be able to focus on work or anything else when it happened. There was also the possibility that it wouldn't take. Perhaps the pills wouldn't fully dissolve into my bloodstream or something and I'd have to do it again.

"How much will it hurt?" I asked. The doctor paused. "It will hurt, it will hurt a lot, but it won't last forever. I have had a patient once ask me to prescribe a narcotic for the pain, but I have never actually had to prescribe something like that." She paused again. She was sitting very close to me. When she came into the room, she complimented my dress. I sensed that she wanted to hug me, but hugging was not allowed anymore. Strange, I never saw the bottom half of her face, but she had beautiful big brown eyes. She continued, "There will be what looks like big pieces of tissue, and that's all it is. It's just tissue. You won't see anything, no fetus, nothing." Another pause, and then "I will say that it hurts more with a wanted pregnancy."

My medication was ready that afternoon, and I knew I would not wait until Saturday to go through with it. I'd already waited long enough. I texted my boss at 9pm: *I am having a miscarriage and as it's very painful and I need time to recover, I wanted to see if I could have the rest of this week as excused or sick days.* I asked my husband for a gin martini.

I waited until 11am the next morning. I laid down an old towel on the bed and put my dog away in another room. I was deathly afraid that one of these little pills would fall out of me without my noticing and my dog would eat it. I don't know what happens if a dog eats an abortion pill, but it can't be good. My husband sat down on the edge of the bed while I inserted the pills, one at a time. I thought I might need him to help me, but it was easier for me to just do it myself. I felt a wave of repulsion as I shoved each pill all the way up. I was repelled by the texture of my insides.

I waited. There was an iPad propped up on some pillows next to me, and I silently watched episodes of *Seinfeld* while tears rolled down my cheeks. I set an alarm for four hours from the moment I'd put in the pills, a countdown to pain.

From my estimates, I expected to start bleeding at 3:30pm, but I was expecting pain to build up to that point.

Hulu has divided *Seinfeld* into "playlists," so you can watch according to various themes within the show. I started on the "Susan" episodes. Poor Susan, agreeing to marry a schmuck like George, only to die licking the cheap envelopes he got for their wedding invitations.

I ordered a sandwich. Still nothing.

I got up to pee, and there was a little smidgen of rust colored blood.

Thirty minutes later, it finally started. It's rare that anyone tells you what a miscarriage feels like. I thought I'd be laid up in bed, clutching my stomach, getting up occasionally to make sure I wasn't bleeding through my pajamas. Instead, I sat on the toilet for hours, doubled over, while clumps of bloody tissue plopped into the water. I couldn't sit all the way up for the pain. I wasn't prepared to feel the sliminess of big pieces of tissue sliding down my vaginal canal. I'd switched to watch *Seinfeld* on the Hulu app on my phone. I watched the "Some Ugly Baby" episode. It was still funny even through the cramps.

Some night, huh?
Some dinner, huh?
Some house, huh?
Some ugly baby, huh?

Every hour or so, it seemed okay to go lay down, but I was always right back in the bathroom a few minutes later. The smell of blood had somehow pervaded the room. I always quickly flushed the toilet without looking too much, but still there was that distinctive sharp and rusty smell. My dog must have noticed it too because he kept coming in and sniffing around every inch of the floor, trying to find the source.

My best friend sent flowers.

My in-laws, having been informed of my imminent loss in the days before, sent nothing. They did not call. I was sitting in the room when my husband told his mother. After a few moments, she changed the subject to how we should know, in case we still wanted to use it, that she had changed their password on the HBOGo account.

After four hours, the pain eased enough that I was able to sit up on the couch. I felt empty, and now I was. I'd done it. I was no longer sitting around with a dead baby inside of me. I continued watching *Seinfeld*. I gulped down the painkillers with a glass of wine.

In Perpetuity

My husband has started putting honey in his espresso, which I find off-putting. I bought the espresso machine last summer, a treat for us when we moved into our new apartment. I commissioned special espresso cups from a ceramicist friend. I love to look at them, these miniature coffee cups. Though I find myself only drinking from our biggest mugs, mostly filled with milk.

I'm used to wearing masks every time we go outside now, but sometimes I still can't understand what my husband is saying. "Big Noth? Who or what is 'Big Noth?'" I ask. "BIG MOUTH, BIG MOUTH!" my husband repeats, louder but still muffled from under his triple layer mask.

My favorite neighborhood bar is a dive on 9th Street and 6th Avenue. It's called Barbès, which I think is a reference to the Paris métro stop Barbès-Rochechouart. While waiting to get another round, I listen to the conversation between the bartender and her friend. "You know what I miss the most?" the bartender asks. "I miss when it was winter and people would leave their scarves and hats behind." "Oh, I know!" her friend replies. "Whenever I'd take something left behind, I'd always lose it almost immediately, like it knew I wasn't its owner."

On the day after Thanksgiving, my husband goes for a bike ride, and I pick up a salad for lunch. When I get home, I am hit by an overwhelming wave of nausea and gag over the trash can. It passes, and I sit down to eat my salad, drink my Diet Coke. When I finish eating, I feel exhausted and lie down on the bed. I open up my phone and look at my period tracking app. I am still three days away from my expected period, probably too soon to take a test. I try to sleep for thirty minutes and then get up and take the test anyway.

I miscarried twice last year and then nada. So I gave up. I took a virtual appointment with a fertility specialist, got ready to try IUI or IVF.

"Holy shit," I text my best friend. I sent her a photo of the positive test. It's a rapid detection test meaning the results will fade within thirty minutes. I pull up my Find My Friends app, looking for my husband's little dot. He's approaching our street. I go downstairs and sit on the front steps of our building, test in my jacket pocket. When he pulls up, I pull out the test and show it to him. He hugs me tight. "I feel a little sorry about drinking so much wine yesterday," I say.

For the first eight weeks of my pregnancy, I go to the fertility specialist to do bloodwork, to look at the baby. Each time I go, *Everybody Loves Raymond* is playing on the TV. Everything measures correctly. Elevated HCG, a fetal pole, a yolk sac, a growing baby, a heartbeat. It seems unfair that all I had to do to get my baby was give up.

These days, when I finally sit down to write, I get distracted. In the Quick Access bar of my Drive, there's a video. It was uploaded by someone named Amelia Johns. I googled her and remembered that I had been in a workshop with her a few years ago. The video that she uploaded is titled "fish unboxing." I click on it and watch twenty seconds of her unwrapping parchment paper tucked around a piece of baked fish.

I have started to stockpile books for my baby. I order books of fairy tales, books I already have copies of but they're still in my childhood bedroom in Mississippi. I feel like I need to read them to prepare.

By the sixth week of this pregnancy, I feel like I am on board a ship in the middle of a roiling ocean. Everything makes me feel sick—the smell of cooking, the smell of my dog, the bright green hue of a cardigan that my husband bought me for Christmas. I crawl out of bed and get dressed so I can appear at work meetings and in workshops, praying that acupressure bands will allow me to get through just this one hour of the day. The only time that I take the bands off is when I shower and then I can see the bruises they leave on my arms. Big purple circles on my veins. I don't think they're doing anything, but what do I know?

When I go back to check my meeting notes, all that I find is "Why do Russians love Aruba?" written in the margin.

My husband is learning French, which I already speak. I listen to him speaking into an app in the next room.

Enchanté. Enchanté. ENCHANTÉÉÉ. Jesus Fucking Christ. Enchanté. Last week, he burst into my office and said, "Is the only word for 'wife' in French 'femme?!' That's incredibly sexist, my woman!"

My therapist wants me to work on confronting the women in my life that I have strained relationships with—a friend who has made different life choices from me, my sister-in-law, my mother-in-law. I said that I would do this, for my baby's sake, but when I wake up the next morning, I think, "Why bother?"

I wish that I was not so attached to my phone. I lose so much time staring at this tiny rectangle. I like Twitter because I log in and have to figure out what people mean when they say "bean dad." My two favorite accounts are Anne Carson Bot and Pépito the Cat. Pépito is a black cat who lives in France. His owners have created a bot that captures and shares every time he goes out and comes back home through his own special door. I press the red heart for every time that *Pépito is home.* The Anne Carson Bot regularly tweets out Anne Carson quotes. My favorite one so far is: *I do not want to be a person. I want to be unbearable.*

Every morning, my husband comes into the bedroom and reports to me a list of each type of bird that he's seen at the feeder while he's preparing the espresso machine. I just want my coffee, but I am pleased by his joy.

I am not afraid of becoming a mom. I am confident that I will raise a good human. What I am afraid of is that by becoming a mom, I will lose myself. For years, I have stressed to my husband that I do not want this to happen, but now it is already happening. I lose hours, days, weeks to laying in bed too sick to move, to read, to think. I wasn't prepared to lose myself so soon.

There is a vent in our bathroom that runs through all of the apartments in the building, all of the smells wafting up to our top-floor apartment. I go into the bathroom to splash water on my face, and I'm hit with the smell of someone's stir fry or cheap fruity shampoo, the brand that used to run commercials of beautiful women saying they needed to stay in to wash their hair.

It's been nearly a year since I've seen any of my coworkers in person. Even though we meet over video regularly, all of the little boxes on screen like the title sequence of *The Brady Bunch*, I'm usually just watching my own little square, seeing what I look like when I speak. I'm tired of looking at my own square, and I miss our weekly meetings where we all sat in the same conference room, and I doodled on a notepad to stay awake. In one of these meetings, the conversation turned to cats, and I piped up, "Did you know that if you die and you're not found right away, the first part of you that your cat will eat is your eyeballs?" There was a silence and then someone said, "Oh my God." That's one of my favorite party facts. My other party fact is that roaches eat your eyebrows and your eyelashes.

Some days, I wake up angry, already in despair at 6:30 am." No, don't start with this," my husband says, pulling on his jeans, while I lay still watching him. "But when will this be over?" I ask, knowing that no one has the answer.

When I go to the hospital for my nuchal scan, the ultrasound technician exclaims, "It's a boy!" She gives me a printed photo of my baby's penis with the word BOY typed next to it. At my OB appointment two weeks later, the midwife said my blood test results would be in next week, but I should let them know in advance if I wanted to know the sex. "Oh, I already know. They saw at the hospital," I said. She looked at me, eyes blank, and said, "We will rely on the blood tests. They're the most accurate." *Okay lady*, I thought, wondering if I should doubt the photo of a tiny penis pinned to my fridge.

We are estranged, in a way, from my husband's family. My husband says that it's not my fault, but last year I published an essay that held up a mirror and there are some hurts that might be too deep to heal. His mother cries and says that my essay was too much, that they already knew how I felt before I published it, so why did I need to write that? That wasn't the point of the essay, I thought, and even now listening to them, I don't believe that they know how I felt. His father said his life experience would blow my graduate degrees out of the water. His words only further accentuated how they didn't know me at all. I had survived domestic abuse, lost my mother at fifteen, moved around and travelled alone through this world as a woman. My father-in-law has never left South Brooklyn.

I go for a walk with my best friend, and she says, "I wish you could see this from the outside, so you could see how much time you are wasting on these people. They're winning because you care so much, but they're not even wise enough to appreciate it." I know she is right, but still, it is hard for me to let it go.

It is Mardi Gras, which reminds me of the last trip that my husband and I took before the pandemic. We flew to Mississippi to see my family and then drove to New Orleans to stay for a few days. My husband saw his first parade one block from our hotel. I took a video of the glee on his face as he watched the marching bands and the floats.

When I was growing up, we celebrated Mardi Gras every year. Every year, I coveted the king cake, asking my mom to cut me a slice. I didn't like king cake; my palate wasn't sophisticated enough for the cream cheese icing, but the green, yellow and purple sugar called to me. The promise of a little baby hidden in a slice called to me. This year, I ordered a king cake for me and my husband. I ate most of it by myself. It wasn't even that good, but it felt like home.

In pregnancy, I start to have vivid dreams. I dream about every ex-boyfriend, every man that I have slept with. When I wake up, I google them to see what they are up to, to make sure they are still alive. I think it's very deranged that the baby boy in my uterus is making me do this.

A friend goes through a breakup, but it's different because she's married and the man who breaks up with her is not her husband. I don't know the rules for this. I have learned how to heal heartbreak (time), but I'm not sure if what I've learned can also apply here. Another friend texts to ask me if my husband and I are still finding it possible to have a physical relationship. "Yes," I say, "but I am also trying to have a baby, so maybe that's different. It's sex with a goal."

I have to remind myself that I am pregnant because when I look in the mirror, all I think is that I am fat. How have I gained so much weight? I wonder. What is happening to my stomach? I look in the mirror and know that these nine months of gestation will probably be no match for thirty-two years of body dysmorphia.

I wake my husband up to say pitifully, "I want a bagel with veggie cream cheese." "Okay, we've got that here. All you have to do is toast the bagel," he says. "No, I need you to toast it."

For the first time in a long time, I cry and say I want my mom. "I feel like no one cares what happens to me anymore," I tell my husband, but I'm not sure if my mom would care either. I start wearing a piece of her jewelry every day—a delicate ring, gold with two tiny emeralds stacked on top of each other. It was given to her by my grandfather, the first piece of "nice" jewelry she ever owned. Now they are both dead.

When I was in my early twenties, I had a strange magnetism for people that no one else would want to interact with—odd people, scary people. They were drawn to me.

My husband says it's because I stare at people on the subway, but really I don't. For years, they would find me, no matter which city I was in. Eventually, this magnetism started to fade, and my walks became less exciting. I assumed it was because I was older; maybe I no longer looked vulnerable or enticing. Recently, though, on a walk with a friend, it started to happen again. First, an older man, walking past me and my friend on 7th Avenue, stopped to ask us if our coffee was any good. We were both holding cups. "Yeah, it's good," I responded, getting a strange feeling. "Well, it's too bad the manager in there is such a BITCH," he retorted, pointing to a coffee shop on the block. Later, sitting on our stoop, a man came up, stared at me with a big smile on his face. "HELLO AGAIN! NICE TO SEE YOU!" he said, beaming. As he walked away, we noticed he was wearing a Frozen backpack. "I've never seen that man before in my life," I told my friend. Not ten minutes later, an intense woman walked down the street, her eyes trained on me. She was older, her white hair streaked with pink, her eyes rimmed with kohl. "What is happening?" my friend said, "this only ever happens when I'm with you." I rubbed my belly. "I think it's him," I said, "he's inherited my one superpower, being a magnet for the interesting and the strange."

I am unmoored. I try keeping a to-do list. I try being kind to myself and only put three things on it: SHOWER, WRITE, READ PROUST AS A TREAT.

It is thirty degrees out, but I am sitting on my stoop with a friend. My butt is numb, but the fresh sharp air feels good to inhale. “It’s like most days, my mind is just blank. I lose hours. I don’t even know what I’m thinking about anymore, maybe nothing. We wake up and every day is the same, and we know there’s a light at the end of this tunnel, but we don’t really know when we’ll reach it,” I tell her. “Are you depressed?” my friend asks. I am staring across the street at one of the stoops that still hasn’t been brushed clean of snow, days after the last storm. “Probably,” I say, “but it’s hard to tell these days whether we’re depressed or if this is just how it is now.”

I used to be afraid when I woke up at 3am, the witching hour. Now I just pee and then stand at the kitchen window eating chocolate chip cookies and wondering if anyone else is awake. Brooklyn looks so quiet now that the backyards are covered in snow. I wonder how long my building has stood here, how many people have looked out this window and seen a quiet snowy night. People standing and looking in perpetuity. Then I finish my cookies and go to lay in bed and stare at my phone.

Home

I did not want to move, or I did but not yet. I thought we would have another year in our apartment, though it was rapidly becoming cramped. I wanted space to breathe, to think, to make things with my hands, and I felt suffocated in the city. Still, I wasn't ready to leave. For ten years, I had clawed my way into belonging here. I wasn't ready to give it up. I just needed a break—a small break from all of the years I had spent here, all of the people I had been before now. Then, our landlord raised our rent.

The movers took two days to disassemble our apartment, during which I had to take my son out of the house so that we weren't in the way. It was June and unseasonably cold and rainy. I had packed away all of his cold weather clothes and had to dig out a sweater and little pants. I had nothing warm for myself, so I walked around the neighborhood in a sleeveless dress. I walked briskly to keep warm, occasionally jogging a bit while I sang to my son. Around and around and around, we walked, treading paths that had become boring to me.

I retraced the first walk I had taken on my own since becoming a new person, a mother. Two weeks after my son's birth via C-section, when I was finally allowed to move more freely, I walked outside, alone for the first time in weeks. I was puffy from the fluids they'd pumped into me at the hospital, slow, sore in my lower abdomen where they'd sliced me open to scoop my baby out. I was unrecognizable to myself. My face was swollen, my body felt alien, I had forgotten what it was like to be alone. I slowly made my way around a single block: 8th Street to Prospect Park West and then back down 9th Street. It was a summer evening and families were out for dinner. A group of young people was walking to the train from Prospect Park. They laughed loudly, limber with youth and booze. I was invisible.

We went to the park on 4th Avenue and 3rd Street where I had to finagle a stroller-seat diaper change. I let my son crawl around in the fake grass until a leering man cackled, "Isn't he cute!" We walked to Community Bookstore, where I bought a new novel for myself and a child's book of mythology for him. My best friend walked over, and we had a coffee together. She gave me an early birthday present, flower bulbs for my new home, for the garden I kept saying that I wanted to start. My son and I went to lunch at a little Italian place with odd hours that my husband and I used to frequent when we first moved to the neighborhood. My son sat in a high chair for the first time, delighted. I took photos of him beaming. I felt guilty because I was moving him away from all of this. It started to rain, and I covered him up and kept walking. I walked the three blocks home, past the gym where I'd gone swimming while heavily pregnant, when I used to leave the pool and walk home in only a towel because it was hot and I was so heavy. When I got home, my dress was soaked, my sneakers waterlogged, and my son was fast asleep. I cried when we went upstairs, and our home echoed with its emptiness.

We had seen the house upstate only once for a brief walk-through. Our decision to leave was quick, and the price was right. I didn't notice that all the old doors were warped and not a single one closed all the way. I forgot that the floors upstairs were checked linoleum, hideous for trying to look like wood. There was no dishwasher, something I was quick to overlook in my eagerness to try a quieter life. The cabinets smelled like earth.

On our first morning in the new house, I got a strange feeling of déja vu. It was my birthday, and I went out to get us coffee. Walking down the house-lined street, I could hear the humming of lawn mowers through my one working AirPod, and I felt like my teenage self again, who had gone for long winding walks through the subdivision where I'd grown up, clutching a Walkman and daydreaming about leaving. To stay was to be lulled into a quiet death, every day the same dull drone of cicadas growing louder until I could no longer hear my own desires. I had to keep walking.

When I got home, the mailman walked up to our porch and handed me a package. It was from my dad. Inside was the title for the pick-up truck that he'd gifted us for the move. I had not driven a car in ten years, and I was afraid of this one even though I'd grown up riding in the back of my dad's truck, gleeful as the wind whipped my hair into knots. In the package was also a letter for my birthday and a wad of cash. The letter said, "I remember you being born like it was yesterday. Here's a little something for your age, plus $4 extra for good luck!" It was $40. I am thirty-four.

At the back of the house is a room that the broker sold to us as perfect for a home office. I turn it into a playroom for my son. It's the first room that I unpack because I need a place to put him down. I mop the floor, unroll the rug from his nursery in Brooklyn, carefully unpack baskets of toys and stacks of board books. Every morning after we sit in that small space for hours, I try to keep him from shoving his pudgy little hands into the heating grates.

My husband, born and raised in Brooklyn, is only acquainted with city wildlife—rats and silverfish and roaches. Within the first week upstate, he excitedly called me from the playroom. "Look! It's a hedgehog!" I looked outside to see a groundhog, beefed up from scavenging vegetable gardens and garbage. He has climbed on top of the fence, surveying his kingdom. A few days later, my neighbor tells me that she saw him in our driveway, shoving his entire body weight into our garbage cans as he tried to topple them.

There are moths everywhere. They fly out of cabinets and flutter through the closets. They perch on the walls of our bedroom. My dog hops onto his hind legs and snaps at them. I complain to the property manager who points out that our lease states we are responsible for exterminator fees. "I will pay for moths incurred," I write to her, "but these moths were not incurred by me." The landlord agrees to pay, and we pack all of the cabinets and closets up again so they can be sprayed. A man comes with poison and makes his way through the house so quietly that I jump when I hear him in the room with me, addressing me as "ma'am." After that, I see only their papery corpses before I vacuum them up.

We make friends with our neighbors. They have a daughter who is seven days older than my son. I watch them toddle around in the confines of a baby jail, and I already know that she will boss him around one day. I wonder if they will be best friends or lovers. Or maybe we will move back to the city and they will forget each other.

On our third day, I stayed up until midnight going through papers and unpacking my office. I shredded ten-year-old papers, appliance manuals for ovens in places where we no longer live, mock-ups of our wedding invitations. Afterwards, I start the water for a shower, and as I remove my makeup, I turn to see that the water is running out onto the floor. The showerhead that my husband has installed is too powerful. It renders the shower curtain useless, the force of the water pushing it aside. A wave of hot water flows out into the hall, down one of the heating grates, into the closet. I am naked and trying to stop the wave with towels thrown down from the moth-infested closet. Downstairs, water drips down from the light fixture in the kitchen. I sink into a puddle of my own, one of defeat and doubt.

In the backyard, I plant a small garden—tomatoes and bell peppers and shishitos. Later, arugula and broccoli and broccolini. I check it diligently, watering it every day, adding nutrients to the soil, but only the shishitos thrive. I bend down to harvest them and see a grasshopper on the netting. Upon closer inspection, it's two grasshoppers, a smaller one on top of a larger one. Grasshoppers fucking over my garden.

My in-laws come to visit, and my mother-in-law says that our new town is just like Staten Island. I bristle. No, I correct her, there's actually a thriving artist community up here. I would never move my son to Staten Island.

My dog goes into the playroom and snarls at a heating grate until I shoo him out. One night, a while later, I am sitting in the dark room, putting away toys, and I hear something scratching beneath me. Something is living under the playroom. I think it is a skunk.

After living in New York City for years, I had forgotten about overhead wires, the ones that make the phone lines and internet connections and electricity run through a grid of houses. How tangled and tacky they look, how dangerous, dangling precariously from an old wooden post.

My best friend and her husband come up for my son's birthday. They help us set up the backyard, prepare the grill, make the birthday cake, buy the booze. My best friend entertains all of the new people I have invited in an effort to be neighborly, getting to know them and making them feel welcome. She is an extension of me. That night, she feeds my son his dinner and puts him to bed because I am so tired. I take a shower and fall asleep by eight. The next morning when they drive back to the city, I cry.

I carefully choose some new pieces of furniture for the living space. A leather couch, a Moroccan rug, two midcentury armchairs that I won in an online auction and my husband drives to Long Island to retrieve. When I arrange it all, I step back and am quiet. "It looks like a mountain lodge from the 1970s," my husband says. Back goes the couch, into the closet goes the rug.

Our landlord is a mystery. We were told that she is a preacher, but there's a mezuzah on our door. She is apparently beloved in the community for being "very spiritual." Our neighbors say that when their daughter was born, she brought them cookies, but they were awful.

I sit on the porch and read whenever I can, clutching my cup of coffee and listening to the muffled noises of my son fussing and my dog barking. I watch the birds in the pine tree out front. The black-capped chickadees are so delicate, their colors so beautifully placed, as if they might actually be made of porcelain. There is a catbird that follows me from place to place, sometimes sitting on a shelf of herbs I've put on the porch, sometimes following me into the backyard, calling out to me. "What do you want?" I ask him, but we don't speak the same language. In an effort to understand him, I research catbirds. I find that catbirds are thought to symbolize facing one's fears, embracing danger and adapting to it. They are also drawn to people who are "embarking on projects where words are important."

My husband takes long bike rides on country roads that I have never gotten to see. I am guiltily resentful of him for leaving the house and having hours of quiet to himself while my mornings consist of making breakfast for the baby, doing dishes from breakfast, letting the baby cling to my legs while the dog whines to be let out again. My husband returns, sweaty and exhilarated, thrilled by the beauty of the outside. "I love it here," he says.

We share the house with spiders. They hide in dark corners upstairs. In the basement, granddaddy long legs lurk in corners, still and quiet. I let them live as long as they don't encroach on my space. When a spider walks across my desk, I brush him away with a block of Post-it notes. The second time he does it, I squash him. My husband takes our vacuum and swooshes up all of the webs in the basement stairwell because he thinks the spiders are scheming to make him walk into their webs. The next day they have just built them back. They were here first, I suppose.

A repairman comes to help install our washing machine. I can hear his voice echoing up from the basement. He is telling my husband about ghost hunting, a hobby of his. "A story that not many people tell is that the guy who constructed the clocktower on the old Dutch church was Jewish, and not only that but he killed himself by jumping off of that very clocktower. His grave is the only one that's facing away from the church." I tried researching this story later. I wanted to know why the Jewish clockmaker was so unhappy that he took his own life, but I couldn't find anything. The graveyard is open and in the middle of town, so I wheel my son around it in his stroller and try to make out which gravestone might be turned away from the church. So many of them are too old, the lettering worn away, and I can't tell the front from the back. One newer stone is for a woman named Kristen who died in 2016. Her epitaph says "She was an old soul," which seems unkind since according to her gravestone, she was only thirty-four when she died. The same age that I am now, standing in front of her final resting place.

I feel more certain that the animal beneath the house is a skunk. At least once a week the smell of skunk pervades the house, waking me from sleep. In the mornings, I see poop that does not belong to our dog. I google "skunk poop" to see if I am right.

I hired a nanny after a month of searching. She has just moved upstate from the city. She's a model, but she's trying to get out of it. We are the same age. She says my name out loud a lot whenever she's speaking to me. "Kaycie, I love this. Kaycie, how do I use the espresso machine again? Kaycie, look!" She hints that she went through a bad breakup with a famous boyfriend but never reveals his name.

A neighbor tells me that they have spotted a fisher cat in their backyard, slinking about and growling. I've never heard of this animal and picture a chupacabra, but upon looking it up later, I actually find it cute, like a big ferret.

I am disturbed to read about its ferocity. Fishers are one of the few predators that target porcupines, darting at them and disorienting them, snapping at their unprotected faces until they stumble. Then the fisher flips them over and disembowels them, devouring their intestines. That night, I dream that a fisher runs into our house. He slinks so quickly about our living room that I can't keep up with where he is. I grab my son and our dog and leap onto the couch, clutching them to me, but the fisher is fast, and he bites all three of us even as I kick him away. My husband is standing in the corner of the room, looking at his phone, searching for information about fisher cats. "We need to go to the hospital," I tell him, still furiously kicking away the fisher. He doesn't look up but finally says, "Ah ha! I know how to trap it. We need to lure it into a garbage bag!" In my dream, we never make it to the hospital.

Flyers go up around our new small town for a fall festival. The festival is sponsored by House of Yes, a venue in Bushwick known for its sexy parties. One of the festival's "DJs for climate change" is a duo I know from my twenties because one of them once gave me molly and took me back to their lounge, which they called the Marcy House because it was situated just outside the J-M-Z Marcy Avenue stop in the still-grungy part of Williamsburg. Standing in front of the flyer now, on a quiet street far from the rumbling J-M-Z train and the din of 2010s house music, one hand on the stroller, the other searching the diaper bag for more baby puff snacks, I feel like my past self is mocking me.

The nanny leaves my son on the changing table, and I find him frightened and half naked. Then she goes off for a long walk while he is sleeping, and when he wakes, she's nowhere to be found. When I gently reprimand her, she starts sending me incoherent text messages about trains and her modeling career. I fire her. A few days later, I come across her photo on a website that I'm browsing for clothes, staring haughtily up at me from my phone screen.

The skunk begins to dig little holes all around the backyard, one of which I trip in while trying to chase after my son and wrangle my dog at the same time.

What was once charming to me about this small town, I now find sinister. I feel like I have been trapped and everyone is in on it. I look suspiciously at others ambling down the uneven sidewalks while I push my son's stroller. They look normal, too normal, as if I'm in a simulation and everyone knows but me. I stop in front of one of the little free library stations, but it is full of books that I would never pick up. The Natasha Tretheway memoir that I contributed is still there, no one has moved it. I sense that it would be possible to lose my mind here.

On a Thursday morning, my husband goes for one of his bike rides before work. I feed our son a waffle with peanut butter, half a banana. I check the time. My husband should be home soon. I open the app that shows me a map, little dots for loved ones, commuting, sitting still, starting their days. This morning, I couldn't find the little dot of my husband. When my phone rings, I seize up.

"I'm okay," my husband says, trying to keep his voice light. "But I've been in an accident and I think I might have dislocated my shoulder." It turns out he broke his collarbone. A squirrel ran out in front of his bike, and he swerved to dodge it and lost control. He flipped over the handlebars, hitting his head. He doesn't know if he was passed out for a while, but his helmet is completely destroyed. He limps up a hill to get a little closer to civilization and call an ambulance and a neighbor to pick him up from the hospital.

I pace nervously until our neighbor pulls up and my husband gets out of the car, pitiful, one arm in a sling, stripped down to the bottom layers of his biking clothes, which are streaked with blood. I am still in my pajamas, hair falling out of a braid and glasses sliding down my nose, baby on my hip. "Thank you," I curtly tell our friend who is carefully hoisting the offending bike onto our porch. My husband limps up the porch stairs. "I think the squirrel lived," he says sheepishly. "I should hope so," I reply.

My husband cannot pick things up, including our son. He cannot make food or wash dishes or drive. I get behind the wheel of our pick-up truck and drive for the first time in ten years to pick up his prescription painkillers. Later that night, I cry while I wash the dishes because I am already so tired.

One evening in early fall, the skunk from under the playroom reveals himself in the corner of our backyard. I wonder if he's sick because it's not dark yet and skunks are nocturnal. He's shuffling, circling his own tail, as if he's trying to make a comfy spot for himself. The next morning, he is curled up on a pile of leaves, and by that afternoon, my husband tells me that he thinks the skunk is dead. Even though his nightly sprays have tormented me for weeks now, I start to cry. A neighbor comes over with a shovel and a garbage bag. Rigor mortis has set in, and it's hard to scoop him up. I cry harder watching from the window as the trash bag is tied and dumped unceremoniously into our garbage.

Sometimes late at night, I hear noises, like someone else is in the building, cooking, walking, living. Only later do I remember that I am the only one who could be making those noises. There are only the three of us, and I am the only one awake.

Age 16

"I just don't think it should have to be so much work." E broke up with me over the phone on a school night. It's true. It was a lot of work, sitting on the phone with him nightly, trying to pull a thought from his brain that I could comment on. A week ago, he'd gotten a boner making out with me on my family's couch and then burped into my mouth. It tasted like root beer.

"Okay, well, I think caring about someone does take work," I said. "Should we still sit together at school tomorrow morning?"

"Yeah, I'm not ready to talk to anyone about us breaking up."

Six months later, E had a new girlfriend, a sweet freshman named Molly. They went to church together. E would still come over to my house. The first time I gave him a hand job, we were laying in my bed, *The Gangs of New York* on TV. The second time, we were in the backseat of his car parked at the abandoned house catty-corner to my dad's. Afterwards, he usually got upset. At least once, he cried. He said there was something wrong with him for wanting this. I thought this intimacy conferred something special on me, both the hand jobs and the crying.

He asked me to go to church with him on Easter, so I did, even though I didn't believe in God and I thought Easter was especially boring. I gathered that he believed this act would grant us forgiveness for the sin of teenage lust. We sat together near the front of the Baptist megachurch that he regularly attended with his family. I was bored but thought he must care about my soul, to be seen with me so publicly. Because I cared about him, I sat through the story of Jesus being resurrected. When it was over, he walked me back to my car. "Why did you park so far away?" he complained.

Age 18-22

I didn't know that our first date was a date. I just thought J was a nice guy and wanted to get to know me because we had mutual friends. I also didn't know that he was actively taking another girl on dates at the same time. I didn't find him attractive, which doesn't explain why I spent five years of my life as his girlfriend.

We lost our virginity to each other when I was nineteen and he was twenty. I drove to Nashville where he was living in a large house with three other men I'd never met. We did it pretty much as soon as I arrived. *Seinfeld* was playing in the background. I laid there, listening to the soft sound of the laugh track. I felt like my insides were being stabbed.

For our one year anniversary, he took me out to a steakhouse. I was a vegetarian. I found out that he'd taken his last girlfriend to the same steakhouse on their one year anniversary. When I asked him about it, he said, "Well, it's a nice place."

He read a lot of books about optimizing your life. The front covers had men smiling with all of their big white teeth, the titles were always in an aggressive neon font. One of these tomes of wisdom recommended keeping a filing cabinet. In it, there should be a folder for every part of life that you need to put effort into, to really think about. While he was in the shower, I looked through his filing cabinet and found a folder labeled "Kaycie." It was empty.

Sometimes, I felt my chest tighten whenever he kissed me, and I would say, "Sorry, I just can't breathe. I don't know what's wrong. I'm sorry."

Four years into our relationship, I was alone, reading in the bath, and I said it out loud, trying it on for size: *I don't love him. I don't love you.* Still, I stayed.

I visited him in Washington, D.C., where he'd taken a job with a consulting agency. We were going to be long distance while I spent a year in Paris to work on my Master's, and then I would join him. I arrived with all of my luggage for Paris and tried to follow the instructions he'd emailed me for taking a train and then a bus and then another train to his office from the airport, but I found I couldn't handle carrying all of my luggage on my own. I called him and asked him to help me. He acquiesced, but he scolded me all the way back.

We went out for drinks with his friends, and one of them joked about how maybe I could aspire to be on one of those "Thirty Hottest Under Thirty" lists in D.C. and maybe do some charity work or something because my degrees were useless. J laughed. I laughed too.

One night at dinner, I asked him to sit on the same side of the booth as me. I wanted to feel close. "No," he said, "I don't want to." When my eyes watered, he looked at me and said, "Enough people really haven't been mean to you in your life."

I didn't want to have sex with him because his room in this new house didn't have a door. It was the basement living space, not meant to be a private room. "Well, you can at least give me a blow job," he said. I wanted him to feel cared about before I left, so I did.

After six months, I called him from my apartment in Paris and said, "I don't think we love each other. I want to break up, but maybe we can be friends." He said, "If you don't take that back right now, I'll never speak to you again." I said, "Okay, bye."

Age 21-23

R gave me letters quoting Ernest Hemingway when I was still in a relationship with J. Of the idea of us together, he quoted *The Sun Also Rises:* "Isn't it pretty to think so?"

When I gently turned him down, he was sad and then angry, and he said he didn't want to be my friend anymore.

We resumed our friendship when I broke up with J, and I told him that, actually, I had feelings for him too. I believed I did, but I also liked my own reflection sparkling back at me from his limerent diseased brain.

He asked me to go away with him for a vacation in his parents' cabin in the mountains, just the two of us. I imagined a week of us reading and talking and fucking. When I got into his car for the drive there, he showed me a cup of marijuana in the console. "What are you going to do with that if we get pulled over?" I asked. "Eat it," he said, and I laughed, but I couldn't tell if he was joking.

He only wanted to watch soccer and play FIFA on PlayStation. I sat on the porch alone, reading French psychological analysis of fairy tale elements and underlining references for my thesis, wondering why I was no longer interesting or sexy to him. He got a cold sore on his lip and complained bitterly that this meant he couldn't kiss me and I needed to go to the store with him right away to get medicine for it. I spent the next two hours consoling him. No, it really wasn't a big deal, and no, I didn't think he was ugly now because of the cold sore.

One afternoon, I missed a phone call from him, and when I called him back, instead of hello, he said, "How is it that you call me back after I have already walked into the library, found a free computer, sat down, typed in my login and opened a Word document? *Then* you call me, and I just have to get up and walk back outside again." I started laughing, but when I realized he was serious, I apologized. "I didn't know you were going to the library to work," I said. "I'm sorry. You can call me back whenever you feel like it."

We broke up over the phone. I cried, and he raged about my inconsideration. How did I think it made him feel? Me crying and making him feel bad when he needed to study for his graduate finals. Is that me caring about him, making him feel bad? He threw his phone into the wall. Then he called me back and said it was my fault that he had gotten so angry that he threw his phone into the wall and now there was a hole in the wall, and he wouldn't get his security deposit back.

A year later, he called me in the middle of the night and cried to me on the phone about how he'd given a girl herpes and now he had to help her pay for the medication. "I'm sorry. . . you gave her herpes? Are you trying to tell me that I have herpes? Why are you calling me about this?" I asked. "No," he cried, "remember the cold sore? That's why I never went down on you. I loved you too much to risk giving you anything."

Isn't it pretty to think so, indeed.

Age 24

T and I met one weekend when I was twenty and staying

in New York City with a friend. The friend had to work, so he asked T to keep me company and show me around the city. I thought he was nice enough and then, for years, I didn't think about him at all.

When I later moved to New York, I knew almost no one, and I thought maybe we could be friends. I invited him to brunch. He was an hour late, but he was so happy to see me again. I put aside my annoyance because I really wanted a friend.

The first time we made out, I was drunk. I had just thrown up and hadn't brushed my teeth.

The second time, he said I should stay at his place because it was so late and it would take me a long time to get back to Brooklyn from Astoria. He made up the couch for me and gave me a spare toothbrush, and when he went to his own room, I left. A man on the train platform joked that he was going to push me onto the tracks. It did take me a long time to get to Brooklyn from Astoria.

The third time, I bought craft beer and expensive lavender shortbread cookies. I chose a movie I thought he would like and invited him to my apartment. We fucked. It lasted two minutes and, after, he said, "I've wanted to fuck you ever since I first met you, when I saw you sitting on the steps at Columbia in that green coat."

He had a sort of girlfriend. I found out when she posted photos of the two of them together and tagged him. The weekend after we slept together, he helped her paint her bedroom and then they went to a wedding together. She worked for a tech company that was in the same neighborhood as the one I worked for, but what she really wanted to do was act. Like me, she had long brown hair. She was pretty, and I looked at the photos of them together and wondered if she was prettier than me.

My best friend found T's YouTube channel and made me sit down and watch it. There were several videos of him and his friend in Santa hats walking around Times Square, talking exuberantly about Santacon. I needed to feel repulsed so that I wouldn't feel sad. After we watched several of the videos, my friend offered to push me down the stairs if there was any possible chance I could be pregnant.

Age 24-25

S was a PhD dropout who loved Faulkner. He was quiet and handsome. He thought he was very funny on Twitter, where his icon was a frog sitting on a rock with its little arms crossed defiantly. He wrote album reviews for Vice. He grew up in Tribeca. We worked together.

He threw a dinner party at his house with all of his close friends. I showed up with a bottle of red wine and no one talked to me. When they all left, he pulled me into his tiny bedroom, a closet under the stairs. I said, "I don't want to have sex with you. It's too soon, and I like you." And he said, "I like you too. We can still make out. And take our clothes off." He slowly unbuttoned every tiny button down the length of my dress. I didn't tell him that I could have just unzipped the side and stepped out of it.

He texted me to meet him at a bar in Williamsburg. His friends were much nicer this time because they'd all been doing coke. S did some more, but did not offer me any. Instead, he pulled me onto his lap. I felt uncomfortable, as if I were a child. I could tell the other women didn't like me, maybe because they thought I wanted to be a sexy baby sitting in their friend's lap. I thought about leaning over to one of them whose name I'd forgotten but knew was something double like Emma Rose or Marie Jane and saying, "I don't normally do this. Sit in grown men's laps," but she never made eye contact with me, so I stayed in his lap and he rested his chin on my shoulder.

When we had sex, I couldn't tell if he just came really fast or he couldn't keep it up on account of the coke. We took a shower together and commuted in complete silence to our office. I told all of my friends about it on our work chat.

He asked me to go to a poetry reading with him. The room was crowded. I'd gotten my flu shot earlier that day so I couldn't tell if it was the room or if my internal temperature was slowly ticking its way up. One of the poets reading was his ex-girlfriend. He didn't introduce me to her but kind of clutched me next to him, so I couldn't escape. I smiled at her, but she didn't acknowledge me. He walked me back to his apartment and said, "You can stay the night if you want," as he walked into his room. "Okay, well do you want me to stay the night?" I asked. "If you want to," he said, laying down on his bed. "Okay, like in here or on the couch?" I asked. "You can sleep in here." I crawled over him, and we both lay there on his twin mattress. By then, I knew that I was running a fever, so I let him pull down my skirt and my underwear. "We're both wearing too many clothes," he said. At 6am I quietly searched for my underwear on the floor and then took the G train home, showered, and called out sick.

He brought another girl to the office holiday party. He got very drunk. When he tried to hug me, I pulled away, but he let his entire body weight fall into me.

Age 25-35

I met D on OKCupid.

After a year, he moved into my apartment. I met his family who overwhelmed me. We got a dog. We moved into a bigger apartment.

I spent many years coordinating: moves to different apartments and one house, ordering paper towels and toilet paper and groceries and soap and laundry detergent, sending birthday gifts to his sister, his mother, his father, his nieces, scheduling vet appointments for our dog, feeding the dog, ordering the dog food and the dog medicine, submitting the dog's vet bills to the pet insurance that I paid for, dusting, doing laundry, changing the sheets, loading the dishwasher, unloading the dishwasher, taking out the garbage, keeping up our social calendar, arranging date nights, paying our bills, dealing with landlords, reminding him of when the Jewish holidays were so that he wouldn't forget to call his parents.

I thought to myself, *So this is what it is to care for someone.*

One night at a dinner, his mother turned to me and said, "You really have to keep up with D's dentist appointments because he's just never going to do that himself."

We got married. We had a son.

I spent many months preparing a nursery: making sure we had diapers and bottles and pacifiers and clothes, researching the best pediatrician, making a registry list, washing and drying all of the tiny baby clothes, making all of the pediatrician appointments and putting them on D's calendar, taking the baby to the pediatrician even after I'd been up all night vomiting, picking out and washing all new clothes every two months as the baby grew, working full-time, asking D for help finding childcare, looking up daycares myself, calling each daycare, interviewing nannies, arranging visits to daycares, choosing the daycare, packing all of the baby's supplies for each day of daycare, holding the baby in my lap during my work meetings on days that we didn't have childcare.

I put my son to bed and had a moment to myself. D walked in and said, "Wanna go fuck?" I did not. The next morning as I was getting dressed, our toddler grabbed my arm and led me to the kitchen to show me something. D was there, making coffee. I was wearing only my bra and a pair of jeans as I poured our son the cup of milk he wanted. That evening D told me that it was fucked up for me to refuse sex with him and then walk around half-clothed, like a tease.

We went to couples' counseling. Four different couples' counselors.

After a session with the last couples' therapist, I asked D why he wanted to stay married to me. "Tell me one thing you love about me," I said. He was quiet for an entire minute before giving me his answer: *You really like art.*

I continued to confirm appointments with the couples' counselor, to put them on his calendar, to follow up each time to ask for the bill so that I could submit it to the health insurance that I paid for.

In the end, I needed to know. I asked, "Why didn't you ever try?" "I just thought you'd always be there," he said.

Age 35

C and I worked together. Two different companies, over ten years of knowing each other. He'd briefly been my manager and I'd long thought of him as a friend.

One night after drinks, we took the same train back to Brooklyn. The man sitting across from us had a large cart and many paper coffee cups crammed in between other things. C leaned over and asked if he could tell me something. "Sure," I said, expecting a joke or maybe a mean comment about a coworker. "If you ever wanted to hook up, I would be down," he said. I turned away from the coffee cups. "Is M okay with that?" I asked, surprised, as I also knew his girlfriend of many years. "I mean, we have talked about it before, but I think it would be more of a 'take it to your grave' thing," he said. "Good to know!" I responded, making brief eye contact with the coffee cup man.

C knew I was separating from my husband and grieving my father, who had passed away a month before. He was my friend. I trusted him.

He took my hand and said, "I can't stop thinking about you," and I said, "That's sweet," both because it was and also because I wasn't sure how else to respond. As he took my bra off, he said, "I looked at LinkedIn to figure out how long we've known each other. It's been at least eleven years." "Hmm," I said, as I gently took over unhooking the clasps on my bra. We took most of our clothes off, and then he needed to get home to his girlfriend.

"When I told you about my marriage, I wasn't trying to insinuate anything, you know that, right? I told you because we're friends," I said to him the next day. I was worried about losing a friendship when I most needed friends.

"I know, but I'm not good at not caring," he responded, "it's part of the intimacy of it."

"I really want to fuck you," he said, "but it's not like if we fuck it's going to be emotionless."

"Right," I said.

Over dinner, he told me about this imaginary world that he and his girlfriend had created over the years. It was vast and had several storylines, and the main characters were a baby and a pig. They did voices for them. "But it's not sexual," he said. "What? That's even worse," I said, after several cocktails. I hated it, and telling me this felt like an even bigger betrayal to his girlfriend than kissing me had been.

Outside, he looked at me and said, "I do have feelings for you, you know." I exhaled my cigarette and said, "Yes, I know." I was careful about the growing hope that my heart was holding for him. I hadn't sought this out.

When we are both in London for work, we fuck. It is not emotionless.

C is racked with guilt after the first night. He asks me to come to his room. I go, expecting to give him a hug and to listen, but when I get there, he pulls me into bed where he squeezes me, restraining my movement and sobs. "I didn't want you to be here," he said, "you're not good for me." He asks if I came to London specifically to sleep with him, to destroy his relationship. I tell him not to speak to me like that, and he apologizes. I comfort him. I tell him that it seems like he's going through some big things and that he needs a support network. I rub his back. He asks me to stay the night, and I do.

All week, in between doing my job and making calls home to my two-year-old, I comfort C. We go for long walks to talk about how hard it is to end a relationship. We sit next to each other at work dinners, and he brushes his hand gently against my thigh under the table. I let my leg rest against his in acknowledgement. I listen to him talk about what he does and doesn't like about his girlfriend. He shows me the texts that she sends him during the week. She says that she loves him and loves their relationship and misses him when he's away. She calls him "my sweet." He asks me what he should say back, and I say that I don't know. I encourage him to call her. He compares her to me several times. He says that he likes that I am naturally beautiful and have aged without having work done. "M cares too much about her face," he said, "she had this expensive surgery done to make her under eyes less puffy." I tell him that I don't think there's anything wrong with caring about your face. I fuck him every night and every morning. I listen to him snore next to me in bed at night. I tell him that everything will be okay. He is my friend, and I don't want him to be sad. He asks who he will be to my son, mentioning the idea of being a stepfather. He asks if I would ever marry again, if I would have another child. I answer carefully. I care for him as if my own heart's not in danger of being broken.

When we return to New York, he calls me to say that he's staying with his girlfriend. He doesn't want to leave her.

He can't see a future with me. "I just had you whispering in my ear all week," he says, while I stand outside in the cold trying to think of what to say back.

At work, he yells at me. He says that he does not want to be alone in a room with me and that there is no reason we should ever need to interact. He says he will do anything to not have to talk to me. It's part of reconciling his relationship, he says. I calmly asked him three times to stop yelling. Finally, in tears, I get up and walk out of the room. The conference room walls are glass. People heard everything.

When it's reported to HR, I protect him. I don't want to file an official complaint. I try to keep him from losing his job. They ask me again and again, "Did he use his position at the company to pressure you to sleep with him?" "No," I say, humiliated. "At any point did you think he might physically harm you?" they ask. "No," I say again. "But he was between you and the door of the conference room, correct?" "Yes, but I walked out of the conference room. He didn't touch me."

He sends me an apology email that sounds stiff and formal and disingenuous. I sign my reply as I do all emails and letters that I send to friends, with only my first initial "—K."

We remain on projects together, but I am instructed to never physically be in the same room with him. Sometimes he laughs at my jokes over Zoom. He talks to me about some of the issues that he's having at work. I start to think we are going to be okay and maybe our friendship can be salvaged. He says that he's sorry for everything.

He resigns and someone else tells me. He throws himself a goodbye party and invites two hundred people. I am not invited. When I ask him why he can't even say goodbye to me, he says, "I can tell you're having trouble moving on and I can't help you with that. I can only help myself. Now that my job doesn't depend on it, I no longer wish to have any contact with you. Best wishes for your future."

"Okay, thanks. Best wishes," I type back.

Acknowledgments

Thank you to Chelsea Hodson, Jenny Boully, Eula Biss, Peter Trachtenberg and everyone at Bennington for your guidance. To Ariél Martinez, Diana Ruzova, Claire Salinda, and Ana Nissan for being my writer people. I am forever indebted to Bennington for bringing each of you into my life.

Thank you to the editors and publishers of *Triangle House Review, No Tokens,* and *Entropy Magazine* where previous versions of some of these essays appeared. A huge thanks to Michael Wheaton who believed in my work early on and has now made this book into a reality.

Thank you to the two people I am perpetually in contact with—Meryl Dakin and Richard Barbieri, early readers who I count on to keep me honest.

To the love of my life, my little Henri Luc, thank you for making me your mom.

To all of my ex-lovers, this is for making me sad. :(

About the Author

Kaycie Hall is a writer and translator from French. She lives in New York City with her son.

— also from Autofocus Books —

Duplex — Mike Nagel

XO — Sara Rauch

Until It Feels Right — Emily Costa

Cleave — Holly Pelesky

Nextdoor in Colonialtown — Ryan Rivas

Too Much Tongue — Adrienne Marie Barrios & Leigh Chadwick

Picture Window — Danny Caine

the nature machine! — Tyler Gillespie

A Kind of In-Between — Aaron Burch

How to Write a Novel: An Anthology of 20 Craft Essays About Writing, None of Which Ever Mention Writing — ed. Aaron Burch

Hiraeth — Mistie R. Watkins

That Spell — Tate N. Oquendo

My Modest Blindness — Russell Brakefield

A Calendar Is A Snakeskin — Kristine Langley Mahler

Culdesac — Mike Nagel

Razed by TV Sets — Jason McCall

In the Away Time — Kristen E. Nelson

The Body Is A Temporary Gathering Place — Andrew Bertaina

Daughterhood — Emily Adrian

A Healthy Interest in the Lives of Others — Teresa Carmody

Yes I Am Human I Know You Were Wondering — Erin Dorney

Leave: A Postpartum Account — Shayne Terry

Out There In the Dark — Katharine Coldiron

Organic Matter — E.N. Couturier

If I Can Be Honest: Selected Prose from the Four Years of Autofocus Lit (2020-2024) — ed. Michael Wheaton

The Dead Dad Diaries — Erin Slaughter

A Revionist History of Loving Men — Lena Ziegler

Marginalia — Naomi Washer

The Third Beat — Lauren Lavín

Tacoma — Aaron Burch

Teen Queen Training: Essays after The Seventeen Book of Etiquette and Entertaining, 1963 — Kristine Langley Mahler

The Father of the Man: The Last Portrait Sitting with Cormac McCarthy — Beowulf Sheehan

What A Hosse Can Hold — Laura Childs Gill